The official inside story

CONGRATULATIONS TO JONATHAN CONNELL, Aged 13, for winning the website competition. He wrote this fabulous poem in honour of Popstars: The Rivals:

Take five sexy girls and five cute guys,
Voices blended to perfection before our very eyes,
A huge pinch of talent, a cupful of ambition, Mixed with blood, sweat and tears: success is their mission,
Top with Louis' expertise and Pete Waterman's skills,
Who will rise to number 1? – it's a battle of wills!

First published in Great Britain in 2002
by Granada Media Ltd
An imprint of Carlton Books
20 Mortimer Street
London
W1T 3JW

In association with Granada Media Group Ltd
Popstars is a London Weekend Television Production based on a format by Screentime Pty Ltd.
Popstars: The Rivals is a Granada Entertainment Production for itv1

Text and design copyright ©Granada Media Group Ltd
Photographs pgs 3, 9 and pg 42 onwards © Ken McKay/Rex Features
All other photographs © Granada Media Group Ltd

ISBN Girl Cover 0 233 05107 4 Boy Cover 0 233 05100 7

Printed and bound in Great Britain by Butler and Tanner Ltd, Frome and London

Project Editor: Gillian Holmes
Design: Jeremy Southgate
Production: Lisa Moore

popstars the rivals

The official inside story

Peter Robinson

GRANADA

Contents

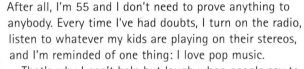

Over the past few months there are times when I've thought to myself, 'Why didn't I just perpetuate the boyband myth and take the easy route?'

After all, I'm 55 and I don't need to prove anything to anybody. Every time I've had doubts, I turn on the radio, listen to whatever my kids are playing on their stereos, and I'm reminded of one thing: I love pop music.

That's why I can't help but laugh when people say to me, 'Pete, you take this all too seriously'. It's life and death for these boys. I don't know about you, but I take life and death very seriously.

I'm not interested in the slightest as to what Louis' lot are up to. I've got something like an 89% hit rate and Louis could never ever compete with me on that scale. I see him spout off all over the place. I'm not in competition with anybody. The kids are. And that's what the show is about.

It's also about good songs. Going back, because I'm an old fart, the power of the good song first made sense when I spent a whole tour on the road with David Bowie. I thought he was the greatest showman I'd ever seen, but I couldn't for the life of me work out how he'd managed to appeal to everyone - from the trendy student crowd, to the party crowd, to the families. It was the songs. They were songs that crossed all boundaries and I realized everything else was bullshit.

By the time you read this, my boys' single will be in the shops, and I'm sure you'll like it. We can't do better than we can do, but we can give it our best. 'It'll do' will never be our attitude - I find that offensive.

In pop, you can never compromise. I make hits - I don't make excuses.

Pete Waterman

Louis Walsh

One of my all time idols is Elton John. A man who spent year after year slogging it out on pub pianos, playing crappy support slots and generally being ignored until he finally hit the big time.

One thing that's surprised me over the course of *Popstars: The Rivals* has been how lazy people can be. This is a tough business. And it's a ruthless business. A lot of the girls I met during the show seemed more interested in their make-up and sunbeds than in working to be a pop star; they had no idea what they were getting into. Some of them just didn't deserve it – so they didn't make it.

I haven't made any secret of the fact that I think the wrong band were chosen as the winners in the first *Popstars*, and right back at the start of these auditions, I knew what I was looking for. I needed a group of girls with the right amount of talent, who were prepared to work hard. Simple as that – but there were times when I was honestly worried about who would be in the final band. As they say, you can't make a silk purse out of a sow's ear.

Popstars: The Rivals has been great fun – the TV team have been fantastic and we've had our fair share of drama. Like the original Nicola, who's no better than a member of Atomic Kitten (and my views on Atomic Kitten are well known!), and who I never would have picked for the band, quitting the show. Then there was Hazel, who I dearly wanted to be in the final band and who I'd still bring back today, who was just a few days too old. It's been amazing, and I've had a ball. But while *Popstars: The Rivals* promises to bring overnight success, it's the bit that comes afterwards that is important to me.

It'll be a few months before any of us know whether we've got the right line-up, though as Christmas approaches I know we're in with a great chance of that Number One. After that, the hard work really begins.

Louis Walsh

Welcome to *Popstars: The Rivals* – **the most sophisticated reality pop TV show in the world.**

Cast your mind back to the year 2000. Scientists announced that the universe was flat, and Japanese police banned drivers from wearing platform shoes after a spate of fashion-related accidents, while Prime Minister Tony Blair's son got extremely drunk in central London. And in the world of music, something happened that would change pop forever.

It is our belief that *Popstars* is the single greatest innovation in television since John Logie Baird thought 'Is there anything on the telly? No? Then I'll have to invent the thing'. Consider the evidence:

Exhibit A: The winners, Hear'say, caused a sensation. Noel, Kym, Danny, Suzanne and Myleene were on every front cover, from *Smash Hits* and the *Sun* all the way to swank reads like *NME* and *The Face*. Their debut single 'Pure And Simple' smashed all chart records, becoming the fastest-selling debut single of all time. Their album, 'Popstars', broke records of its own and gave the band a second number one single with 'The Way To Your Love'. A sell-out arena tour was followed by a second album and single, both called 'Everybody'. While this book was being written, Hear'say announced that they had split, and the cynics who led the media hate campaign against the band had, sadly, won. It's a reminder to the eventual winners of *Popstars: The Rivals* that while success may come overnight, the real work has only just begun.

Exhibit B: In happier news, the runners-up, Liberty, got themselves a record deal with jumper-wearing uber-businessman Richard Branson. An unknown funk act also called Liberty got in a huff, so Tony, Kevin, Michelle, Jessica and Kelli renamed themselves Liberty X and scored a string of hits, including the huge Number One 'Just A Little' and massive follow-up 'Got To Have Your Love'.

Exhibit C: Another star of *Popstars* was a young man called Darius Danesh, who shocked the country with a frankly unpleasant 'interpretation' of Britney Spears' '...Baby One

More Time'. By summer 2002 his beard was gone ('Hoorah!' – everyone), and as a direct consequence he scored his first UK Number One with 'Colourblind'.

Exhibit D, E, F: The judges. TV bigwig Nigel Lythgoe, label talent-spotter Paul Adam and pop manager Nicki Chapman quickly established themselves as stars in their own right, with Lythgoe in particular earning himself the 'Nasty Nigel' tag for comments such as: 'If you think you can sing, you're either deaf or stupid'. (Precisely none of the entrants were deaf, so draw your own conclusions.)

For a show planning to launch just one band, *Popstars* unearthed a lot of talent. This time round things are a bit different, reflecting the different ways the *Popstars* idea has been altered around the world. In Canada, for example, the first series put together a girlband (Sugar Jones broke records all over the shop), then came *Popstars: Boy Meets Girl* with its unisex pop troupe (the oddly named Velvet Empire). And, as you read this, Canadians are watching *Popstars: The One*, which is looking for the new Eminem!

And here the case rests.

Back in the UK, *Popstars: The Rivals* is the most elaborate version of the show on the planet, a complex game of one-upmanship in which two of the most significant figures in pop battle it out, and the UK's premiere pop princess attempts to stop World War 3 breaking out. Here's the plan:

Step One: Pete Waterman, Louis Walsh and Geri Halliwell separate the wheat from the chaff.

Step Two: The general public eliminates any further wheat bearing any resemblance whatsoever to chaff, leaving two bands. The girl wheat will be taken under Louis' managerial wing, while Pete will steer the boys.

Step Three: The bands release their debut singles on the same day aiming for the Christmas Number One. The upper reaches of the charts are a 100% chaff-free zone.

Step Four: Pete and Louis never speak to each other again.

This book is the story behind *Popstars: The Rivals*, and the bands battling it out as Santa starts dusting down his sledge. But it's also the story of those who didn't make it, and the collective highs and lows that have made unmissable TV for four months.

The tears and laughter, the wannabes and never-gonnabes – they're all here, and we've been given exclusive behind-the-scenes access to the gossip, interviews, tantrums and private moments you didn't see on TV. And some of it will pop your eyes right out of your head, so if you're a spectacle wearer clean the inside of your lenses.

Welcome to *Popstars: The Rivals*. Let battle commence...

Planet Popstars!

Over 35 countries have had their very own *Popstars* bands – here are just a few...

Australia: Bardot and Scandal'Us

Girlband Bardot were the first act in Australian history to have their debut single and album at Number One at the same time. Scandal'Us, from the second series, followed them into the record books.

Italy: Lollipop

In 2001 the girl group's debut single 'Down Down Down' went straight to Number One! Then went down down down. Ho!

USA: Eden's Crush and Scene 23

Five-piece girlband Eden's Crush enjoyed international success with debut single 'Get Over Yourself', though Scene 23 went pear-shaped when their record label closed down earlier this year. Bummer!

Denmark: Eye Q

Trine, Louise, Sofie and Julie won the show and released 'I Want What She's Got', followed by an album, 'Let It Spin'.

South Africa: 101

The mixed five-piece's 'What's It Gonna Be' was the fastest-selling Number One for a debut single in South Africa's chart history!

Rivalry in History

David vs Goliath

David was a normal boy. Goliath was a giant, with a beard. David whooped Goliath's ass. (As Darius noted, people with beards rarely win.)

Blur vs Oasis

Oasis released 'Roll With It' on the same day as Blur's 'Country House'. Blur won the battle due to Damon's chiselled good looks, and the fact that 'Roll With It' was a bit of a turkey.

Napoleon vs Wellington

The feud between Napoleon and Wellington is one of the most fascinating conflicts in history. Pete Waterman remembers it well.

The Beatles vs The Rolling Stones

If The Beatles were around today, they'd be a1. The Stones would be Ash.

Spice Girls vs All Saints

Geri's crew sold 28m records around the world. All Saints made combat trousers quite popular.

Stalin vs Trotsky

The Russian political bigwigs never got on, though that's what happens when you spend all day drinking vodka.

The godfather of pop
Pete Waterman

'Writing rock songs is easy. Great pop takes talent.'

As he'll be the first to explain, 55-year-old Pete Waterman is one of the most important men in the history of modern pop music.

His no-nonsense attitude ruffles feathers, but he's been fluent in the language of pop for more than a quarter of a century, responsible for around 500 million record sales. Or 5,000,002 if you include Jason Donovan's later efforts. Two years ago he published his autobiography *I Wish I Was Me* – a rags-to-riches tale in which his passion for steam trains was laid bare. We'll spare you the details. We caught up with him during the auditions.

How quickly can you make your mind up about someone in an audition?
'I can make my mind up in 30 seconds. If you've been doing this for 30 years and you don't know after 30 seconds, you're wasting your time.'

What will you be looking for in the prospective Popstar?
'I do these auditions totally differently from everyone else because I don't take any prisoners and that sometimes makes me unpopular with the other two judges. For me it's voice, voice and voice.'

What about the look?
'I don't care what they look like or what shape they are or what their dancing's like. When they start to talk about image and all that rubbish, that's when I find it difficult. I can't get my head round this "we need a blonde one and a dark one" business, I just want to find great singers.'

Which songs are you sick of hearing?
'Well, I never thought that Alicia Keys song "Falling" was very good, but after these auditions it's even more boring. The boys have been singing Enrique Iglesias' "Hero" a lot, just because it's an easy song to sing. That don't impress me much.'

Is there any danger of 'audition fatigue'?
'I'll have to keep my eye on Geri and Louis because they're finding it incredibly hard work. I've had to gee them up at times, but that's because I know you've got to stay alive at all times. If you don't stay sharp you've lost it.'

Have there been any Darius-types this time round?
'There ain't no Darius this time round. We have had a few who were in *Pop Idol* or *Popstars* and that's great because they're giving it a go, but there ain't no Darius. He was a one-off, totally unique.'

Do you ever get any abuse from any of the contestants?
'Nah. You joking? They're far too frightened of us.'

Pete's greatest hits

Kylie Minogue: Debut single 'I Should Be So Lucky' was written in three minutes as a teenage Kylie sat in Pete's waiting room.

Steps: Rescued pop from the brink of extinction. Key lyric: "A smile's a frown turned upside down." How true.

Dead Or Alive: 'You Spin Me Round (Like A Record)' is the third best single of the 1980s. Pete produced it.

Princess of pop

Geri Halliwell

'As long as you're a good person and you have integrity, you will always get what you deserve.'

1998: In May, Geri leaves the Spice Girls. By October she's signed with EMI for a deal reportedly worth £2m, and has been appointed Goodwill Ambassador for the United Nations. She sings 'Happy Birthday' at Prince Charles' 50th.

Geri should be familiar with the role of peacekeeper – she spent four years in the Spice Girls, after all! With that band a distant memory for many new pop fans, it's easy to forget their all conquering importance in late-90s pop, spearheaded by Geri's defiant 'Girl Power' manifesto. In fact, Geri's ideology empowered an entire generation of girls like no artist since Madonna. Here's how...

Geri Halliwell: a beginner's guide

1972: On August 16, Geraldine Estelle Halliwell crashlands on Planet Earth.

1984: Dyes hair for the first time.

1990: Geri makes the first of several early bids for fame. Over the next few years she'll try everything from topless modelling, to being a hostess on a Turkish gameshow.

1994: Answers an ad in *The Stage*, which asks 'Are you streetwise, ambitious, dedicated?' She's one of five successful applicants, and joins the band: Touch. They change their name to Spice and join Simon Fuller's 19 Management, signing to Virgin for an estimated £2m.

1996: Geri becomes Ginger Spice as the Spice Girls' debut single, 'Wannabe', spends seven weeks at Number One and six months in the Top 75, topping charts in 31 counties. Their debut album 'Spice' goes platinum six-times in six months and is the UK's biggest-earning album of the 90s. By the end of the year they've signed over 40 product endorsement deals, worth £5.5m.

1997: 'Wannabe' is the highest ever entry by a debut act on the US Billboard Hot 100; they become the first UK group to hit Number One with their debut. The band win two Brit awards, their *Girl Power* book is translated into 20 languages, and 'Mama' makes them the first act to hit Number One in the UK with their first four singles. Geri pinches Prince Charles' bottom. The band sign a deal with Pepsi and release their first movie, *Spiceworld*, then a Number One album of the same name. They end the year, once again, at Number One.

1999: Geri's debut solo single, 'Look At Me', is released, kept off Number One by... Louis Walsh's Boyzone. Her album, 'Schizophonic', hits the charts and two Number Ones ('Mi Chico Latino' and 'Lift Me Up') follow, as does an autobiography. *If Only* becomes a bestseller, shifting over half a million copies.

2000: Geri appears from between 50ft inflatable legs at the Brit Awards, performing another Number One, 'Bag It Up'. Later she speaks at a UN Summit For Children conference and upsets Catholics by dancing erotically with a back-up singer dressed as a priest!

2001: 'It's Raining Men' hits UK Number One followed by Geri's second solo album, 'Scream If You Wanna Go Faster'. Geri's yoga guide becomes one of the surprise hits of the year as she flies out to Oman to entertain British troops.

2002: With a second book, *Just For The Record*, in the bag, Geri takes up golf, unveils her new waxwork at London's Madame Tussaud's, and signs up to be a judge on some show called *Popstars: The Rivals*...

The Judges

Louis Walsh

'I couldn't do a rock band because they bore the pants off me.'

If you've got Louis Walsh on your side, luck doesn't come into it. He has one of the sharpest business minds in pop management. After years on the management circuit he made his name in the 90s with Boyzone and Westlife, while this decade has seen huge success with the likes of Samantha Mumba, Bellefire, legendary pop diva Lulu, and Ronan Keating. In 2001 and 2002, Louis was a judge on the Irish version of *Popstars*, and led the winning act Six to Ireland's fastest-selling debut single of all time. But don't be fooled by his calm, fatherly exterior – Louis can be as ruthless as they come...

Have you learned anything from the first *Popstars*?

'I don't think about Hear'say because I would never have picked that band. Apart from Myleene. I like Liberty X though, because they've had two great songs.'

What are you looking for?

'The whole package. The attitude is almost more important than the voice. You can have the best voices in the world but if you don't all get on it's no good to anyone. And I have to like them! If I don't there's no chance the public will.'

What sort of attitude are you looking for?

'They have to understand they're getting a chance in a million. This lot will be getting everything overnight, but they have to work for it and be thankful because it can go away as quickly as it came if they're not nice to everybody.'

Which songs are you sick of hearing?

'Anything I like, because so many of them were being murdered. Shakira's being murdered a lot, and there are a lot of bad Blue versions. But it's good to hear Ronan and Westlife, I think they've been the most popular songs - which I like!'

How are this lot comparing with Irish *Popstars*?

'Well, the Irish one was done on a total shoestring, and we worked 24/7 to get it done. This one is much more professional, we've got a great team and that makes it a lot easier.'

Are the other judges behaving themselves?

'Geri and I agree to disagree with Pete a lot of the time. There have been a few crossed swords along the way. We have to make sure that we're keeping the right people - nobody is going to make it through the net unless they're totally right.'

Would you like to see someone Irish in this group?

'I would, absolutely. There is one girl I think will make it all the way, and a guy called Peter Smith who got down to the last 12 in the Irish *Popstars* who has gone for this one and I think he is very, very good too.'

Louis' greatest hits

Boyzone: Ronan Keating, Stephen Gately and three builders enjoyed massive worldwide success, mainly with ballads.

Westlife: Started off sitting on stools. These days the record breaking quintet stand up a bit, with eleven Number Ones in the bag.

Samantha Mumba: The R&B diva has conquered America with a blend of urban sass and good hair.

The toughest judges around...

The British Public

The public's greatest hits of democracy

Tony Blair: Voted into power in 1997. Sweats quite a lot, but running the country's a tricky business sometimes.

Brian Dowling: Millions voted Dowlo to win 2001's *Big Brother*.

David Beckham: Voted BBC Sports Personality Of The Year in 2002. 'It is amazing,' he mused at the time.

There are around **59,755,700 people (of whom you are only one) living in the UK,** which averages roughly 588 people per square mile. Jack and Chloe are the most popular names for children, and marriage rates recently rose for the first time since 1992, which is good news for people who, like Pete Waterman in his early years, run wedding reception disco outfits.

And introducing your host...

Davina McCall

'I don't have to break any bad news. I can just be lovely to everyone!'

Davina's greatest hits

Big Brother: 'This is Davina. Do not swear!'

Don't Try This At Home!: The exclamation mark in the title is totally justified for this elaborate, Davina-hosted dare show. Creepy crawlies and tall things featured largely.

God's Gift: This 1995 late-night dating show featured Davina attempting to maintain order as a troupes of scantily-clad men attempted to impress The Ladies. Not for the faint-hearted!

Since her first big break on MTV, 35-year-old Davina has become one of the most recognised faces on British telly. She has a string of high profile presenting jobs under her belt, including *Streetmate* (the Channel 4 dating show),*Big Brother* and the 2000 Brit Awards. In 2001 she presented the live final of the first *Popstars* series, making her the perfect choice for *Popstars: The Rivals*! Also in 2000 she married *Pet Rescue*'s Matthew Robertson, giving birth to their first daughter Holly Willow in 2001.

Above: Davina always makes time for a chat.
Right: Lisa Riley's new haircut fooled nobody.

The Auditions

A breezy day in July begins much like any other for thousands of youngsters up and down the country. Cornflakes are spilt down school blazers, bosses tap their watches disapprovingly on the factory floor. Then gradually, word begins to spread: auditions for *Popstars: The Rivals* have been announced. Stardom beckons once again. It's time to fill in applications...

The plan's simple: auditions will take place in London, Manchester and Glasgow. As it turns out, extra dates are added as unexpected numbers of hopefuls, from the daring to the demented, turn up to perform for Geri Halliwell, Louis Walsh and Pete Waterman. Thousands will be sent home immediately — some upset, others furious.

For those who pass the auditions, this is just the beginning. Of the 112 hopefuls accepted for the callbacks in London, only 77 will go through to the next day. And the numbers keep dropping — to 50, then 30. Then 20. Finally, after the voting public have had their say, just five boys and five girls will remain.

But let's begin at the very beginning: Sunday, August 4 in the bleak wasteland of north London...

Queue the music

One hopeful shows off her invisible monkey

Part of the rigorous age-checking process

It's fitting that the road to fame starts at Wembley. For many popstars, playing Wembley Arena is the ultimate goal, but for the London wannabes trying their luck over the next four days the venue is the rather less legendary: Wembley Conference Centre. Each day, through the snaking queues, the air is crackling with nervous tension. Once they've signed up at the front desk, there's a holding room where auditionees wait for their moment in the spotlight. Every so often a member of the production crew will clatter through the door and bellow something along the lines of, 'L121 to L130, follow me please!' Complete gibberish to the untrained ear, but for ten auditionees it's the voice of destiny. It's showtime!

For some, the situation is eerily familiar. One of the first to face the judges is Essex lad Taz, a star of the first *Popstars* series. He made it through to the final 30 and has decided to dust himself off and try again. 'I feel as if I've learned a lot since the last *Popstars* experience,' he admits. 'I reckon I'm in with a pretty good chance.'

Unfortunately for Taz, his confidence is a little misplaced and the judges knock him back immediately. He's absolutely gutted. 'It just didn't happen,' he tells us with a shake of the head, as he leaves the audition room. 'It didn't go well at *all*. Louis said he didn't like me at all and Pete was just rude. Pete's just trying to be Nasty Nigel all over again. It's pathetic. But I'll be back. Mark my words.'

Twenty-three-year-old Andrew Kinlochan is next up in front of the panel. The softly-spoken Will Young lookalike has chosen 'Lately' by Motown legend Stevie Wonder for his party piece, but isn't sure if it's the right song. 'I'm not too happy with it,' he explains, 'but I haven't got time to change it now.' Five minutes later and it seems he did pick the right song after all. 'I really mucked up the beginning and I had to start again,' he cringes, 'so I'm quite surprised they let me through. Geri was really nice to me.' Hurrah!

During a breather, Pete and Louis stop by for a quick chat, and it soon becomes apparent that Pete hasn't quite got his head round the new-fangled fashions these young folk are sporting. 'One lad turned up with oil on his jeans!' Pete splutters. When Louis Walsh slowly points out that in some circles distressed jeans are considered fashionable, Pete roars, 'I don't care about all that. Even I had a shave and put a clean shirt on today!' Bless.

Lee King, 19
Song: Simon and Garfunkel, 'Bridge Over Troubled Water'
I was more worried about singing in front of Geri, Louis and Pete than singing in front of the cameras, but they said I wasn't right so that's the end of that!

Gos, 23 *(left)*

***Song: Holly Valance, 'Kiss Kiss'** I was out with my mates in Sheffield last night and we were talking about these Popstars auditions, and I lost a bet which meant I had to travel down on the coach and go for the auditions! It's just a bit of a laugh, but I got to dance with Davina which was cool.*

Geri's made quite an impression on the two veteran starmakers. 'She's so funny,' laughs Pete. 'She said two things today that made me spit my tea everywhere.' And as for their search for a star, they're confident. 'I haven't seen a Darius or a Gareth yet, but I may have seen a Will,' says Pete.

And the auditions continue. Things take a turn for the argumentative with a young guy called Paul Rose. Geri and Louis think Paul's great. Pete, who'll be managing the boyband, flies off the handle to such an astonishing degree that the *Popstars* cameras have to stop rolling. There's a happy ending as Paul is allowed a second chance to sing, and makes it through to the next round.

Somebody else to disagree with Pete is feisty Chloe Staines, who also makes it through and is so brimming with natural confidence that she immediately holds an impromptu press conference when she leaves the audition room. Must be something about the colour of her hair – and if we've got our first Ginger, then here comes Baby, in the shape of 16-year-old Jamie Lee Church. The blonde youngster sings 'Just A Little' by Liberty X, and immediately goes through to the next round. 'My throat went dry just before I

Anton Gordon, 19

***Song: R Kelly, 'I Believe I Can Fly'** I only decided to come down to the auditions yesterday, but I live round the corner so it was pretty handy. I've heard people say that Geri's been a bit hard but I thought she was the nicest of the lot. Now I'm here I want to go all the way.*

started,' she squeals, 'and Pete gave me a glass of water to make sure I was okay. I only sang about a sentence before they stopped me and said, "You're through". I'm really happy.'

Davina spends a lot of time chatting with nervous mums, settling nerves, offering a shoulder to cry on and celebrating with the winners. She's more Big Sister than Big Brother. At one point she stops to talk to Claire Soutar from Norfolk, who is decked out in pink. 'Pink's my signature colour,' says Claire grandly. '*I* want a signature colour!' wails Davina.

Emma Beard is celebrating. She's been up since 6am but the early rise hasn't dampened her spirits 'cos she's strolled into the next round. 'I had an instinct I might get through because the camera crew seemed to follow me all morning,' she grins. 'When I walked into the room, Pete, Geri and... what's the other guy called?' Ahem. Louis Walsh. 'Oh yeah. Anyway, Pete and Louis were really chatty but I was slightly intimidated by Geri. Still, I thought, "I'm here to prove myself for me and my family", so I decided to go for it. I just want to hug my mum!'

Hug duly dispensed, Emma's mum tries to take in the madness of the London auditions. 'I just want Emma to have a good time and have some fun,' she says. 'If she gets through to the group it'll be her dream come true.'

The dreams won't take shape for a while yet. After an exhausting few days in London, the judges are packing their bags, hopping on the train, and heading up to Manchester...

Above: The godfather of Pop holds court
Right: Don't think much of your 'Elvis lip', mate

Who on earth chose that carpet?

The nerves set in

Has it been good news for Aimee Kearsley?

New auditions, new city – new swank location. In refreshing contrast to the bleak Wembley Conference Centre, Manchester's Lowry Hotel is a designer hang-out with its own share of celebrity guests, from J Lo, Kylie and Westlife to Lord and Lady Beckham.

On the first day, Pete Waterman trudges out for a chat to the hundreds in the queue. 'Don't sing any bleedin' R&B,' he barks at a group of girls. 'I'm sick of it. Sing something poppy.' A few faces fall. 'Um, what about Celine Dion?' whispers one girl. 'Yeah, she'll do,' shrugs the Hitman. 'What time is it now, 10.30am? You'll get in about four'. How's that for a pep talk?

Pete grabs us to vent even more complaints. 'If I hear another lad singing

Aimee Kearsley, 16
Song: Dina Carroll, 'This Time'
I made friends with about six girls in the queue and we were all singing to psyche each other up which made us all feel a bit more confident. I came to audition for the TV show Model Behaviour last week, but this is what I really want to do.

Ronan Keating in an Irish accent I'm going to throw up!' Ah, it seems like the rivalry between Pete and Louis is bubbling away nicely. By now, Pete's branded Louis 'a complete idiot', while Louis has hit back, with 'Pete's a nice guy but he's living on past glories. He doesn't know what young kids want.' Time will tell.

Seventeen-year-old Manchester lad Shane Ward faces the judges early on – singing 'If Tomorrow Never Comes' by Ronan Keating. Oh dear. 'Pete Waterman didn't like me,' Shane says. Funny that. 'In fact, he said he didn't think I had a cat in hell's chance of making it through to the band. The other two disagreed and they persuaded him to put me through to the next round. I just told Pete that I'll try to prove him wrong.'

Sixteen-year-old Esther Taylor from Darlington has a cunning plan. She sings 'Venus' by Bananarama, which was produced by one P Waterman. And sure enough, she gets through to the next round. 'I thought he might notice me if I sang one of his songs, and it seems to have worked.' Genius! But if few girls have chosen 'Venus' as their audition song, we're absolutely certain there aren't many guys who will be auditioning with the choice of a guy called Danny – he's gone for camp classic 'I Am What I Am'. He exits the room in floods of tears. Davina offers a lovely shoulder to cry on. 'They said I was an entertainer but I'm just not right for the group,' he sobs. Poor lad.

Pete's got half an hour to spare, so he stops for another natter. 'There are some kids who stand out straight away and some who you miss,' he explains. 'Will Young nearly passed me by. He was a scruffy bugger and when he walked through

Russell Graham, 17

(left) *Song: Westlife and Lulu,
'Back At One'*
**Louis Walsh told me the song
I sang was his favourite song,
which I was pretty pleased
about! Although Geri told me
to stop waving my arms
about! It's such an unreal
experience, especially after
watching the first Popstars.**

the door. I only put him through as a sympathy vote.' Blimey.

No such doubts for Pollyanna Woodward, though – she's through to the next round. Even so, the 20-year-old model from Nottingham is still quaking! 'My legs haven't stopped shaking all day!' she grins. 'I sang "Just A Little", and Louis Walsh was fantastic to me. He really wanted to put me through. Pete and Geri were a bit unsure at first, but they came round, thankfully!'

Pete Waterman's stepped out of the audition room again, looking a little more subdued than normal. 'We've just seen someone who's sensational. If you think Gareth Gates had a quirky story, wait 'til you see this guy.' He's talking about 16-year-old Liverpool lad Andrew Coleman, who's virtually blind. 'I couldn't talk for two minutes,' Pete smiles, 'and Geri was crying. He's through to the next round.'

But stop! Who's this walking through the door in a Union Jack dress, ginger wig and frightboots with ten inch platform heels? It's Essex girl Sarah Belsey, of course. 'I've always been a huge Geri fan so I thought this would be the perfect way to meet her,' she tells us. 'I've got no idea what she's going to say when she sees me. They're

Sarah Belsey, 22

Song: Spice Girls, 'Wannabe'
**I'm not exactly sure what
Geri will think of me, but
hopefully she won't be
too mad! Either she'll laugh
or be really annoyed,
but I'm only doing it for a
laugh. There's been a really
good atmosphere in the
queue, everyone's been
singing along.**

either going to burst out laughing or she's going to be really annoyed. I don't even know what I'm going to sing yet.' You'd better make your mind up quick, you're on in five minutes!

In other Geri news, Josh Wilson is recovering from a bit of a shock. He was in the men's loos practising his song, as you do, when Geri walked in. The real one. That's right, into the men's loos! Closely followed by the camera crew. Quick, zip up! 'I didn't know what to think,' Josh laughs. 'Geri heard me singing "I'll Never Break Your Heart" by the Backstreet Boys and wanted to investigate. It was all a bit weird.'

As another round of auditions come to a close, Louis has a few choice words about Pete. 'He doesn't know what he's up against,' he growls. 'Pete's band will be Number Two but mine will be Number One. And as for lads singing Boyzone or Westlife songs, I think it's great. The only reason Pete is annoyed by that is because no one's singing his songs any more. He's old news.'

Pete, predictably, has his own opinions of the Manchester crowd. But surprisingly, they're favourable! 'Y'know what, kids in London are too cool for their own good. Kids in Manchester, they're so polite. You tell them they've not made it through and they say "Thank you." They don't take it too seriously.'

Don't take it too seriously? Does he not see the rejected, weeping masses lining the streets of Manchester? But there's no time to dwell – once again, the judges pack their bags, and head further north...

*Above: Mikey is oblivious to the presence of true pop talent
Right: Isn't there anything else on the telly?*

Jamie and Chloe check out the competition

Keith goes mean 'n' moody

"It's amazing! It's a window! With a sign in it!"

For this, the final stage of the *Popstars: The Rivals* **audition process, we move north – to Glasgow's Royal Concert Hall.** This will be base camp for just two days, but we'll still have our fair share of characters.

The set-up is familiar to the judges, but while the hopefuls down south limbered up with group renditions of Alicia Keys or R Kelly tunes, the auditionees up here are getting into the spirit of things by singing a throaty number called 'You Cannae Shove Yer Granny Off A Bus'. It's got Number One written all over it. (FYI: The general opinion is that you cannae shove yer granny, 'cos she's your mammy's mammy.)

Davina is wandering around the holding area, reprising her role of Big Sister and dishing out advice to worried auditionees. 'If they say anything nasty to you,' she begins, 'don't worry.

But try to ask them for some constructive criticism so that at least you'll take something from the experience.' She shares secrets from behind the scenes at *Big Brother* (Brian's her favourite) and even tells a group of girls what went on during her hen night (she went mountain climbing in Snowdonia with three girlfriends, believe it or not). One girl asks how the *Popstars: The Rivals* experience compares to other shows she's presented. '*Big Brother* was mad,' Davina laughs, 'but this is even madder.'

The first person through to the next round from the Glasgow auditions is 18-year-old Alan Burgeon from Aviemore in the Highlands. Alan's a chef, but has wanted to be a singer all his life and claims he knew every word from *Grease* by the age of two. Quite an achievement, and it does the trick – he's through to the next round!

Pete's on usual vitriolic form. 'One guy sang (Motown classic) "I Heard It Through The Grapevine",' he splutters, 'and it was truly terrible. I said to the poor lad, "Can you hear that noise? It's Marvin Gaye spinning in his grave".' Billy Warren from Wishaw is one of the few to impress the legendarily acid-tongued Hitman. Billy is another veteran from the original *Popstars* series and this time sings 'Show Me The Meaning Of Being Lonely' by Backstreet Boys, which Geri told him was her favourite song. 'I had only got halfway through it when Pete stopped me, turned to me and said, "There's no doubt you've got a brilliant voice – in fact it's one of the top ten voices we've heard in all the auditions"! I was pretty chuffed. They advised me to maybe try to lose a few pounds, which I thought was a bit cheeky!'

There are more than a few eyebrows raised whenever Dublin girl Hazel walks by. She seems more mature than the rest of the crowd, and she's a lot larger, given that she's seven-and-a-half months pregnant! If she gets through, it'll mean she gives birth just as the final line-up is announced to the world, but that hasn't stopped her flying to Glasgow to try out for the girl band. She jumps the first hurdle (metaphorically, of course, for she is with child), and gets through to the callbacks.

There are no auditions in Ireland, so there are plenty of hopefuls here who, like Hazel, have crossed the Irish Sea. For a few of them, like 17-year-old Christina McQuillan from Belfast, the first girl to make it through to the callbacks, the journey has been worthwhile and she's rather excited about it. 'Everything is going mental!!!' she gushes. Yes, it really is three exclamation marks' worth of gushing. 'My world is just spinning round! It's so overwhelming! I can't believe it! I was just so excited to see Geri and the other two, I thought, "I can't believe I'm standing in front of famous people!"'

Christina tells us that after the audition, Louis called her back and asked if she was from Northern Ireland. 'But he said that wasn't the reason they put me through,' she adds. That's funny – Louis has already told us that he would love to have an Irish girl in his group! 'Of course I want someone Irish,' he said, adding with his usual modesty that 'Let's face it, the Irish are better at everything in this business. They're better singers, they're better dancers and they're better behaved. And that's a fact.' Good job Pete Waterman didn't have his hearing aid in!

Peter Smith knows all about Louis Walsh. The unassuming Dubliner made it through to the last 12 of the Irish *Popstars* series. 'I don't listen to anyone who says this is pressure,' he says. 'This is a bit of fun. Pressure is waking up with six kids and a mortgage and no job.' Wise words indeed. Pete's a top guy and he deserves to go all the way this time round.

As the auditions roll to a close, the judges know that, between these tryouts and those in London and Manchester, they have already met the five girls and five boys who'll be battling it out for Christmas Number One.

It will be three unpredictable and emotional months before they are finally identified...

Peter Smith, 23
(right) Song: Ronan Keating, 'When You Say Nothing At All'
I got the 7.30am flight over from Dublin this morning so it's been non-stop. I was fortunate to get through to the last 12 in the Irish Popstars show but didn't make it into the band Six so I thought I'd give it another go. There were 5,500 people who entered the Irish Popstars so I was delighted to make it to the final 12, I wasn't disheartened about not making it all the way. I'll never give in, that's the fighting Irish for you!

Chris Woods, 19 *(left)* Song:
Aerosmith, 'Don't Wanna Miss A Thing'
I broke my leg in a drunken nightclub experience in Portrush – my friend fell on it when we were a bit tipsy. It happened about a month ago but I get the plaster off next week so it didn't stop me going for the audition. I missed last year's Popstars but I was working in Majorca as part of a Steps tribute band – I was Lee. I don't think I'll be singing a Steps song, I'm sick of them now!

Above: "Waiter! We ordered forty minutes ago!"
Right: Davina explains the finer points of bio-organic chemistry

The girls go for Number One. (Number two's not pictured, fortunately)

"This song needs more basin it." Now wash your hands

It's five days since the final round of auditions in Glasgow. But for those singers talented, lucky, or pushy enough to be invited through to this next stage, there's still no guarantee of success – especially since a significant proportion are nursing hangovers from last night's ill-advised booze 'n' karaoke sessions back at the hotel. By the end of today's callbacks at London's Imperial College, 35 people will be sent home.

The 112 successful auditionees from London, Manchester and Glasgow find themselves in a huge hall, all seated in a neat square. Pete, Louis and Geri sit in front. All 115 people are facing the stage. It's like the school assembly from hell. And so the process begins: one by one, they take to the stage, sing in front of the black background made famous by Darius' '...Baby One More Time' atrocity, and return to their seats.

When they deliver a belter the place goes wild – for example Paul Rose, who caused uproar in London when Pete refused to consider him for the boyband, triumphs with Boyzone's 'No Matter What'. But for some, like Alan Burgeon from the Glasgow auditions, the pressure to perform in front of over a hundred other starlets-to-be is too much. And when things go wrong, the silence is deathly.

Some are lucky to get anywhere near the stage – Stephanie McMichael has left her birth certificate at home, and like the rest of the hopefuls needs it to prove her age to the Popstars crew. While she waits for her brother to fax the document through, the judges allow her to perform her tune, an astonishing version of Ike and Tina Turner's 70s classic 'River Deep, Mountain High'.

Louis loves it, but by lunchtime Pete's having doubts that any of this lot will be up to scratch. Geri agrees – and reckons she knows how to solve the problem. Calling a halt to the auditions, she turns round to address the assembly and leads everyone in a 'primal scream', which is Geri-speak for a load

Scream if you want to go further!

of yelling. Of course, Pete takes to it like a natural.

There's a noticeable improvement during the afternoon, with Pete describing Peter Smith from the Glasgow auditions as 'one of the best singers I've heard'. Praise indeed – don't forget this is the man behind Jason Donovan. And still they file on stage, sing their songs, and shuffle off. But finally, as the day draws to a close, everyone's had their turn and the judges retire to consider the performances, knowing that one third will have to go. After an hour, they emerge from the bunker...

'Well', Pete begins. 'We're very disappointed by today.' Faces fall. 'Those of you coming through tomorrow will be expected to up your game by at least 500 per cent.' All 112 hopefuls are now on the stage – boys on one side, girls on the other – and as the rolecall of names begins, they leave their groups on either side of the stage and join the swelling gaggle in the middle.

By the time the judges have finished, nobody's sure whether it's the group in the middle, or the remaining boys and girls on either side, who'll come back tomorrow. Inspecting the groups, it's easy to appreciate the confusion, as there are strong contestants all over the place. Jonathan and Yewhan Baker, the brothers who'd made such a strong impression on Davina, are in the middle – but Paul Rose and Peter Smith are at the side.

And after a difficult day, the judges seem to enjoy keeping them in suspense for those few extra seconds. Pete breaks the silence. 'Those in the middle... We won't be asking you back tomorrow.' Either side of the rejects, the

stage erupts. As the unlucky ones filter out of the hall with a shake of the hand from Pete and Louis, for those remaining, dreams of Popstar Rivalry become a little more real.

Bye for now!

Chris Tame, Raquel Lee, Rachel Hemmerman, Joanne Fogatt, Esther Taylor, John Norton, Jessica Mitcheson, Christopher Tolley, Jeni Harding, Zoe-Denise Smith, Jonathan Baker, Yewhan Baker, Ema Dane, Natasha Bates, Marcus O'Donovan, Damon Valentine, David Pilkington, Chris Turton, Claire Huckle, Bryn Christopher, Bill Wan-en, David Gourlay, Victoria Pierson, Steven Archibald, Kigelah Tunani, Ryan Taylor, Ross Taylor, Jem-Lee Mocock, Ashley Andrews, Stephen Blackie, Oyana Walsh, Kelly Magee, Rachele Williams, Jamie-Lee Church, Justin Webb.

Tania helps Andrew get to grips with a dance routine

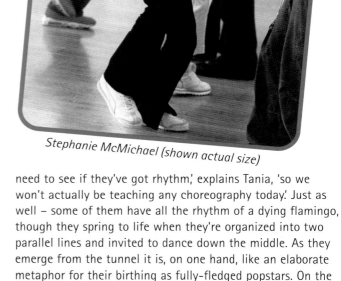

Stephanie McMichael (shown actual size)

Day two at the Imperial College. Twenty seven will go home today. First, however, some good news for one would-be popstar: after (though not as a result of) a sleepless night in the hotel bar, Jeremy Metcalf is now the proud father of a bouncing baby boy. 'It still hasn't sunk in!' he tells us. 'In a way I feel like I should be with my baby, but my fiancé Kelly's told me to stick with this.' So he does. Davina breaks the news to the 76 other hopefuls. 'Drinks are on you lot!' yells an over-the-moon Jeremy.

But here, the fun must cease. For there are international pop ambassadors to be found. Time to bring in the dreaded tutors... First there's Jo, vocal tutor to the likes of Ms Dynamite and Craig David. ('But they can sing!' you wail. Well that, you see, is the point.) Then there's Tania, twinkle-toed choreographer for everyone from Will Smith to the mighty Liberty X.

While the introductions are being made, Geri blusters into the production office with a man on her mind. Nothing new there, then – but this time it's Justin Webb, a cute, blonde-haired boy who was kicked out yesterday afternoon. 'Ah yes,' Louis says mysteriously, 'he reminded me of Stephen Gately.' Well, Geri reckons they've made a mistake – so he's given one more chance, and invited back. Fortunately he only lives around the corner. Downstairs, the dancing's in full flow. 'We just

need to see if they've got rhythm,' explains Tania, 'so we won't actually be teaching any choreography today.' Just as well – some of them have all the rhythm of a dying flamingo, though they spring to life when they're organized into two parallel lines and invited to dance down the middle. As they emerge from the tunnel it is, on one hand, like an elaborate metaphor for their birthing as fully-fledged popstars. On the other hand it's 77 people leaping about like loons. Geri feels for them and gives one of her legendary pep talks, explaining how, even when she was in her prime, she'd still be terrified of dance routines. 'Look at Gary Barlow,' she adds. Though of course we can't, because he's not here. (He didn't even get through the auditions.)

By now, Justin Webb's turned up for his second chance. Today he is wearing a hat, which seems to go

Jacob Thompson

'I haven't seen much of Geri, even though she was so keen to put me through! She's been watching us and pointing a bit, writing a few things down then walking out of the room! I found yesterday and today quite tough – I've struggled on the singing part of it and I find it really difficult to sing on my own in front of everyone. The nerves start kicking in, man!'

Javine Hylton

'I don't get nervous when I'm dancing, and singing in groups relaxes you a bit. As for the tuition, they want to be able to mould the boys but I don't think they could do that with the girls – a lot more of us already have experience in this profession so we know our stuff. I'm glad Louis is the one who picks the girls – he's lovely, but Pete isn't open to anybody else's views but his own!'

One trailerpark girl goes down the inside, down the inside, down the inside

down quite well.

He gives Geri, Louis and Pete a private performance – Pete gets the '500 per cent improvement' he was after yesterday afternoon, and Justin's back in the game.

During a break in the proceedings, we find Paul Rose, the boy who'd been responsible for Pete and Louis' massive bust-up at the auditions. 'Today I'm more relaxed,' he confides. 'Tania's brilliant and she's bringing out the best in me which is fortunate because I've never had any dance lessons!'

For Paul and his fellow rivals, the day flies past until, once again, the group is split in three. This time, it's those on the outside who are unlucky. It's a tough call, and Andrew Coleman, the virtually blind entrant who brought tears to Pete's eyes in the audition, is one of those not to get through. As the days go by and the chance of getting through to the final band seems closer, so the pain of rejection becomes ever more acute. The stress is also taking its toll on the judges, and the end of the process is still months away.

Peter Smith

'I know that Louis has said he would like to see someone Irish in the band, but it's going to be difficult. There's very few of us, for one! And there are so many talented people here too. But to be honest with you, I've got no right over anyone else to be in the group, because everyone's been through the same thing. I just hope everyone gets something from the experience because it's a decent bunch of people.'

Now go, walk out the door:

Richard Agacy, Carrie Richards, **Noala Farrelly,** Nyima Symone Small, **Elissa Friday,** Raphaelle Fouett, **Paula Jade,** Andrew Coleman, **Chris Yardley,** Shavne Ward, **Matthew Hucknall,** Karen Tomlinson, **Andy Newbury,** Alicia Gee-Pemberton, **Bryan Nisbet,** Russell Graham, **Marcus Birks,** Katie Miller, **Danny Kinge,** Samantha Atkinson, **Jeni Beadman,** Stephanie McMichael, **Leveme Scott-Roberts,** Alan Burgon, **Loma Grant,** Dawn Petticrew **and Thomas Spratt.**

New dad Jeremy gets baby tips

Tutor Jo points to a high note

Behind closed doors: the moment of truth

Today, as yesterday, there's an early start: up at 7.30am, meet in the hotel foyer at 8.15am, get to the college by 9am, and straight down to business. With less here than yesterday the rooms are beginning to seem a lot bigger and, in an act many hopefuls consider to be a major romantic obstruction, the boys are separated from the girls. During the morning, the boys will be concentrating on vocals, and the girls will be dancing. After lunch, they'll swap over.

The boys are given 'Til There Was You', a fairly obscure Beatles song that provokes various comments along the lines of, 'Can't we do Westlife?' and '"Livin' La Vida Loca" would be a bit easier'. 'The songs I'm picking are there to challenge the boys,' Pete booms. 'We already know they can sing Ronan Keating – there'll be a lot who can't handle this.' He's right. The boys only have an hour to learn the song and practise it once before running through under the four beady eyes of Halliwell and Waterman. 'I can honestly say,' Paul Rose honestly says, 'that I've never been so scared.' The afternoon's session for the girls is rather less stressful – they're given S Club 7's 'Never Had A Dream Come True', a song tattooed on the very psyche of a potential popstar.

Before they know it, it's green mile time; a sight familiar to viewers of the first *Popstars* series. As it happens, the queue is neither green or a mile long – it's white as a sheet, and made up of just fifty people waiting to hear whether they'll be performing at Wembley or sweeping its floors. One by one, they enter the room and find Louis or Pete behind a desk. For thirty of them, the news will be good. We catch a quivering Owen Doyle before he goes in. 'It's been difficult seeing people go through the week,' he explains. 'But I've been lucky so far and I've made some good friends. I'm praying to God we're all here at the end.' As it turns out, God is in an obliging mood today – and Owen gets through.

Less lucky is Paul Rose. He was right to be scared. 'Right from the auditions they've been waiting for me to slip up,' he says glumly. 'Now Pete's booted me out. But I've learnt so much from this. Hopefully when the *Popstars* show has run its course I'll get my career going.'

We hope so, too. And for the thirty who've got through today's ordeal, there's still a long way to go – they're coming back tomorrow morning. And ten of them will get the boot.

Just Turn Around Now:

Darren Pounds, Nina Landoli, **Louise Emmanuel,** Fiona Merry, **Kerry Pitt,** Bevan Pughsley, **Natalie Clarke,** Paul Rose, **Rebecca Gordon,** Lee Pitchford, **Shannon Bowen,** Craig Alien, **Victoria Curtis,** Scott Whittaker, **Paul Tapscott,** David Wheeler, **Jakie Latu,** Martyn Anthony King, **Michael Wooife,** Danny Kelly **and Christina McQuillan.**

Hazel hits the big time.

24 Hour Party People:

Peter: *'Owen's the worst at staying up late, he's had a few late nights.'*
Owen: *'But even then it's only been 1.30am, that's not bad!'*
Jamie: *'I've always been in bed before 12, honest! Well, maybe not last night... Anyway, Chris is the worst at sleeping in. He got the fright of his life yesterday morning!'*
Chris: *'Thing is, I arranged for a wake-up call and it didn't go off. Then my mobile rang and I jumped out of bed and realized what time it was. Everyone was already at the dance studio! I can't believe no-one came and knocked on my hotel room. Call themselves friends? Well, I consider them more associates, haha!'*

Though rejection at this stage will be a disaster – and today, ten singers must indeed hit the dumper – there's a sense of relief as the 30 hopefuls roll up this morning. Ten boys and ten girls will go into the Popstars houses, but the remaining ten will be kept in reserve in case any of the chosen 20 need replacing. Like, if they turn out to be ten days too old, or throw a diva strop and quit the show, or anything like that.

The day involves another round of singing and dancing, and very little in the way of drama. 'Everyone here really wants it,' explains Javine Hylton. 'And they want it badly. We're putting 500 per cent in, and now everyone's personalities have come though. We're becoming individuals.'

Javine also chooses today to big it up for Geri. 'She thinks about us all the time and her heart's in the right place for everyone,' she adds, while Chloe Staines agrees that, 'You can see she's concentrating really hard on this. I think she's quite a brilliant person, really.' Taking a breather during the afternoon, Jamie Shaw tells us that he's already prepared for the hard work that might lie ahead. 'This job is 24 hours a day, seven days a week,' he admits. 'And Pete's been saying, basically, if you're not committed, please leave now. But I'm ready for that. When he says work, you work. There's no messing around.'

There's no messing around for the judges, either. For Pete and Louis, the decisions they make today will make or break their reputations in the music industry. To give themselves some more time, rather than tell today's final thirty today whether they're through, they'll be making personal visits over the next two weeks to thirty individual homes. Mother – get into that loft and fetch the best china!

Geri checks out the talent with Pete's assistant, Helen

You're Not Welcome Any More:

Jeremy Medcalf, Jacob Thompson, Justin Webb, Sean Haven, Pollyanna Woodward, Annika Gabbitas, Kimberley Walsh, Charlie Hewson, Nicola Roberts and Owen Doyle.

Anton Gordon

Before *Popstars: The Rivals*:
Like George Michael and Elton John, Anton has two first names. The 19-year-old lives with his brother and two sisters in leafy Neasden and has taken a year out from a sound engineering course in favour of *Popstars: The Rivals*. Anton's won loads of local talent contests and counts Coree from Damage as a cousin – could his natural, soulful talent run in the family?

Why will the boys beat the girls?
We'll deliver the best vocals, and attack that track!

What are your chances of being in the final five?
Two in ten. (thinks) Well, hopefully I'll get through. It's the public vote I'm scared of!

Who's been your champion on the judges?
Pete has given me a lot of confidence along the way. Louis gave me a couple of compliments, too.

What scares you?
Not making it as a singer, and having to work a 9 to 5.

Who do you fancy out of the girls?
All of them. Cheryl's definitely the popular one with us guys, and Emma. But they're all gorgeous.

If this fails, what's Plan B?
Just do more auditions. Hopefully something will come out of this. I'd like the five who don't get in to form a band of their own.

Emma Beard

Before *Popstars: The Rivals*:
Emma applied to the big theatre schools – RADA, LAMDA and the rest – but they all rejected her, like big fools. She'll be19 during the course of *Popstars: The Rivals*, and remembers feeling oddly calm when she attended the auditions, confident that she'd follow in the footsteps of musical heroes like Whitney, Alicia Keys and Ms Dynamite.
Emma does not actually have a beard.

Why will the girls beat the boys?
We'll have the better package all round, I think.

What are your chances of being in the final five?
I was really shocked, to get this far, but as I've got into the final ten, I think, 'Oh, maybe I could get into the five now'. We'll just see.

Who's been your champion on the judges?
I'm sure Louis liked me from the start. Deep down, my gut feeling is that Geri liked me too.

What scares you?
Spiders. They're just creepy and ugh!

Who do you fancy out of the boys?
None of them!

If this fails, what's Plan B?
I'll be completely gutted! But I'll just keep on going for it, to show people I really can do it.

Mikey Green

Why will the boys beat the girls?
Well, girls will fancy us for a start. And we'll be better, obviously.

What are your chances of being in the final five?
I've always had confidence in my own vocals. I'm confident in my ability. I think I'll be okay.

Who's been your champion on the judges?
Louis has given me some nice compliments and Geri's really energetic and inspiring. But Pete's my boss.

What scares you?
Not succeeding. I set myself high targets and it's awful not to get them.

Who do you fancy out of the girls?
Sarah's really good looking. And Cheryl.

If this fails, what's Plan B?
I'd go back to writing songs and singing in bands. Not sure if I'd go through this again, ha ha!

Before *Popstars: The Rivals*:
Think Mikey looks like David Beckham? Someone obviously did – the 22-year-old Chorlton boy once worked as a Becks lookalike, in between catwalk jobs, walk-on parts in shows like *Hollyoaks* and ad shoots for companies such as JD Sports. A keen musician, Mikey gigged all over the place as lead singer for three years in a band called Myan. He has a personalized number plate on his Peugeot 306.

Lynsey Brown

Why will the girls beat the boys?
I want to prove to Pete that we're better. Some of the tracks Polydor have given us are fantastic, too.

What are your chances of being in the final five?
Everyone in this house deserves to get in. I've got as good a chance as everyone.

Who's been your champion on the judges?
I didn't think any of the judges liked me, but I suppose they must have done and I'm very grateful!

What scares you?
Spiders. That's all.

Who do you fancy out of the boys?
I don't fancy any of them at all. They've got great personalities, though, I suppose...

If this fails, what's Plan B?
I'd go through it again because this is what I want to do. There'll be so many doors that open through this.

Before *Popstars: The Rivals*:
Lynsey comes from Little Holton near Manchester and lives with her brother, sister and mum, whose front room Lynsey recently redecorated. (All went well, though Lynsey admits she's totally accident prone!) When she moved into the house she still hadn't told Salford University that she wouldn't be enrolling. Lynsey reckons she can be bossy from time to time, and likes to keep things tidy. Crikes!

Matt Johnson

Before *Popstars: The Rivals*:
Matt is 17. At 13 he played a lead in *Les Miserables*, and went on to star in a touring production of *The Famous Five* with Jon from S Club. Later on he realized his dream and played Oliver in a production with bald unfunnyman Russ Abbott, and even sang for the Queen when she visited his school! He also sang in pubs and clubs and auditioned for *Pop Idol*. He was too young, but made a lasting impression on Pete Waterman.

Why will the boys beat the girls?
The majority of people buying singles are teenage girls! And Pete's better than Louis – he's creative, whereas Louis is a marketing person.

What are your chances of being in the final five?
One in two. It's as easy as that.

Who's been your champion on the judges?
Geri's spoken publicly about me – she loved my moonwalk and said I was her favourite!

What scares you?
Spiders! Drowning's quite scary, too.

Who do you fancy out of the girls?
Nadine's nice. But any will do, ha ha! Lynsey. Nadine's got the nicest bum.

If this fails, what's Plan B?
Wait to see if I get any offers or anything, and then give a few friends a call, see what happens.

Nadine Coyle

Before *Popstars: The Rivals*:
Derry-born Nadine was already a familiar face to Louis Walsh – she'd auditioned for Irish *Popstars*. In fact she made it into the final band, only to be rumbled at the last minute for being too young! Fortunately, at 17 she's old enough for *Popstars: The Rivals*. In Derry, Nadine performed in various pantos (including *Sleeping Beauty* in the lead role!) and sang covers in local pubs.

Why will the girls beat the boys?
We've got better songs, we're better looking and we've got a better record label.

What are your chances of being in the final five?
I'm not going to be there! Well hopefully I will be, but I'm not that confident about it.

Who's been your champion on the judges?
It's difficult to know what they've said behind closed doors – hopefully all of them!

What scares you?
Death, mice and rats, and the pitch black dark – this house is scary in the dark! It's like *The Shining*!

Who do you fancy out of the boys?
None of them. Sorry!

If this fails, what's Plan B?
Well, I won't have lost anything, so I'll just try again and get back in the saddle.

Andrew Kinlochlan

Why will the boys beat the girls?
We'll be better. I've heard us all sing together. We're gonna do it.

What are your chances of being in the final five?
The public could take against a small thing about you, something so slight, and kick you out!

Who's been your champion on the judges?
I've never been quite sure! But recently Pete's been really good.

What scares you?
The dark. I've always been scared of the dark!

Who do you fancy out of the girls?
Javine's the nicest looking, she's got everything that's right for the group.

If this fails, what's Plan B?
If I literally got nothing out of it, I'd go on holiday for a month, then come back and start again.

Before *Popstars: The Rivals*: Listing Stevie Wonder and Mariah Carey as his favourite artists, 23-year-old Hertfordshire boy Andrew hasn't had a huge amount of public exposure – he got down to the London finals on *Pop Idol* and enjoyed college performances and karaoke turns, but until recently was working as a hotel admin manager, whatever that might involve. He enjoys shopping and playing the saxophone, though rarely at the same time.

Sarah Harding

Why will the girls beat the boys?
We're all about ten times better looking and we've got so much more personality, enthusiasm and our voices are just like the bomb!

What are your chances of being in the final five?
I'm not going to jinx it by saying!

Who's been your champion on the judges?
At one point Geri came over and started saying, 'Come on! You can do this!' Louis is just a cheeky Irishman! He's quite warming.

What scares you?
Having to go back to really awful jobs.

Who do you fancy out of the boys?
No comment!

If this fails, what's Plan B?
I really want to be in the band – but there are plenty more opportunities out there, at the end of the day.

Before *Popstars: The Rivals*: Sarah had a difficult time at school following a move from Staines to Stockport, and left when she was 15. Before long her main hobby – karaoke – led to a career singing covers in pubs and bars, though a stint in a girlband ended before they released their first single. Now 20, the rally car buff has worked for a debt recovery agency, which she says will help her deal with tricky characters during *Popstars: The Rivals*.

Nikk Mager

Before *Popstars: The Rivals*:
Nikk is 18, and was born in Halifax. The town, not a branch of the bank. Nikk's already had a few near misses with fame: he made it to the final 50 on *Pop Idol*, the final five on *Star For A Night*, and almost got into a boyband put together by Hear'say's management company. Being not ugly, Nikk was also crowned Model Of The Year 2002 by radio station Galaxy 105. Warning to the squeamish: he picks his toenails.

Why will the boys beat the girls?
We're better! Louis just goes for manufactured acts.

What are your chances of being in the final five?
No idea. I'd like to think I'll survive the first week, though. It's up to the public!

Who's been your champion on the judges?
Pete's been great recently.

What scares you?
Death! And paparazzi, though they're only doing their job.

Who do you fancy out of the girls?
All of them! My favourites are Cheryl, who has amazing eyes, and Emma. I like brunettes.

If this fails, what's Plan B?
I haven't even thought about it. I'd keep going, keep plugging away, and try again. I'll be at the next audition! You will see me again!

Javine Hylton

Before *Popstars: The Rivals*:
When she was 18, Javine scored the role of Nala in the West End production of *The Lion King*, which she reckons is one of the greatest achievements of her life. West London-born and bred, the 20-year-old loves going to garage raves and has recently been working with producers on her own music, which has an urban, All Saints flavour. She lives with her sister and mum.

Why will the girls beat the boys?
We've got more to give. Boys have two left feet, and we've just got everything.

What are your chances of being in the final five?
100%. Definitely. I'm so different to everyone here. I just stick out I think.

Who's been your champion on the judges?
Geri – she understands where we're coming from, so she takes care of our needs and how we feel.

What scares you?
Not having my make-up in the mornings! (Guffaws)

Who do you fancy out of the boys?
They're a bit too boyish for me. I like a man! Justin Timberlake would do nicely.

If this fails, what's Plan B?
I don't think it could fail, to tell you the truth. I know I'm good, and something will come out of it.

Chris Park

Why will the boys beat the girls?
Girls aren't as good as boys, for a start. And none of them can dance as well as me.

What are your chances of being in the final five?
One in two. But if the public see me for who I am, I'll be in with a good chance.

Who's been your champion on the judges?
Pete didn't like me at first, but Geri talked him round, which I'm grateful for.

What scares you?
Failure.

Who do you fancy out of the girls?
I love Cheryl to bits, she's perfect.

If this fails, what's Plan B?
I've got lots of plans – B, C, D, E and F. But they'll only be revealed if they need to be. Watch this space!

Before *Popstars: The Rivals*: 20-year-old, Newcastle-born Chris has already experienced life in a pop group – Xpoze. (Check out that crazy boyband spelling!) They toured with the likes of Blue, Liberty X, Steps and Samantha Mumba, but recently split, leaving Chris to work as a legal advisor and lay down tracks in his spare time. As a youngster he was a keen ballroom dancer, and appeared on *Stars In Their Eyes* as pop nutter Adam Ant!

Aimee Kearsley

Why will the girls beat the boys?
Girls are a lot closer than the boys. We can show more emotion and gain a connection. I don't think the boys are going to be hugging each other and holding hands!

What are your chances of being in the final five?
It's very difficult to say that because every single girl in this ten now is just as talented as me.

Who's been your champion on the judges?
They've all been great – Geri's been nice, and Louis seems kind and gentle and really understanding.

What scares you?
Spiders! I could never, ever touch one.

Who do you fancy out of the boys?
I like Daniel.

If this fails, what's Plan B?
I'll carry on, this is good exposure for all of us so I'm sure there'll be a happy ending.

Before *Popstars: The Rivals*: Having attended an all girls school for the past few years, 16-year-old Aimee's well-prepared for any clashes in the house. Aimee loves going out (preparation can take up to two hours!) and lives at home in Stockport with her mum, dad, sister and twin brother, Adam. Aimee was due to start college this year but then *Popstars: The Rivals* came up and, well, you know how it is...

The Final 20

Before *Popstars: The Rivals*:
Already an accomplished performer, Daniel has performed backing vocals for the likes of Craig David and drummed his way around the smoky jazz clubs of London and Kent, often as part of his band, Rain. At 24 he's the oldest of the final ten and has had his fair share of dodgy jobs - working as a waiter and at one point last summer even slogging away in a factory putting the tops on lipsticks!

Daniel Pearce

Why will the boys beat the girls?
(Laughs) If the five guys I think should be picked are picked, there's no contest.

What are your chances of being in the final five?
I'd hate to say! 50%.

Who's been your champion on the judges?
Initially Pete wasn't going to put me through! But Geri butted in.

What scares you?
Not succeeding in music. And not making my mum and dad proud.

Who do you fancy out of the girls?
Javine, definitely. A lovely, stunning, down-to-earth girl. She's really chilled out.

If this fails. what's Plan B?
I'll go back to my drumming and songwriting, and session work. I'll make a living whatever happens.

Before *Popstars: The Rivals*:
17-year-old Nicola swapped her college course for *Popstars: The Rivals*, even though she didn't actually want to apply, and only relented when her family insisted! Nicola's pop career to date involves local charity work (including singing for the NSPCC) and a spell in girlband Devotion.
Nicola replaces: Nicola Ward, who cleared off in a right old huff. Good luck with your glittering career, Wardy!

Nicola Roberts

Why will the girls beat the boys?
The girls have got that bit extra! The boys are just the same day in, day out, and people will get bored.

What are your chances of being in the final five?
We're all as good as each other. Which means that now it's just down to fate.

Who's been your champion on the judges?
Louis wasn't at the start but he likes me now – and Geri's been behind me all along, which is nice.

What scares you?
I'm really jumpy, Halloween is a nightmare for me! The house is terrifying too – surrounded by forests!

Who do you fancy out of the boys?
I already have a boyfriend so none of them interest me. Jamie's got a nice personality though...

If this fails. what's Plan B?
Carry on. I'm sure something will come along.

Keith Semple

Why will the boys beat the girls?
It comes down to how well we perform. We'll win.

What are your chances of being in the final five?
They're good. Simply because I've got experience in bands playing instruments, and I'm used to touring.

Who's been your champion on the judges?
Geri liked me from the first audition. They've all been nice, and Pete's really got to know me well.

What scares you?
Nothing – I take everything as it comes.

Who do fancy out of the girls?
Chloe! She's absolutely beautiful. She's very smart, and more like a woman than the others.

If this fails, what's Plan B?
Continue with my band. We were doing very well anyway and as long as a I can play to people somehow, that's fine.

Before *Popstars: The Rivals*:
21-year-old Keith is an avid sportsman and has been writing songs since he was 12 years old. His first band, Aarc, formed in 1997 and recorded an album. After school Keith paid the bills by forming Klass, gigging up and down the country performing covers from the likes of Abba and Van Morrison. Keith's hoping *Popstars: The Rivals* is second time lucky as he got down to the final 100 in the first series...

Chloe Staines

Why will the girls beat the boys?
They're just going to be sat there singing on stools, but we're going to be funky, fresh and happening!

What are your chances of being in the final five?
I'm a good singer and dancer. I'm also hoping my personality will act in my favour.

Who's been your champion on the judges?
Geri's been really complimentary. She said I'm really pretty, and I'm a great package, which I'm grateful for.

What scares you?
Being murdered.

Who do you fancy out of the boys?
I don't fancy any of them!

If this fails, what's Plan B?
Carry on. Even if I don't get into the band I will just do everything, anything I can to focus on my career and get it started.

Before *Popstars: The Rivals*:
By the age of 12 Chloe, who lives in Essex with her mum, sister and two brothers, had already been on TV (with Esther Rantzen) declaring 'I want to be famous, and I will be famous'. More recently she's appeared in pop videos (including one for indie art rockers Lamb), and her face appears all over London in billboard ads for the kids photocard. Though she's 18 now so of course doesn't qualify for one.

Jamie Shaw

Before *Popstars: The Rivals*: Like Danny from Hear'say, Jamie made an early appearance on ITV's *My Kind Of Music*, and even scored a record contract as a result. Things went a bit wonky when, at 14, his voice broke, but he used the money from the deal to build a studio in his house. Now 17 and with his voice back on form, Jamie enjoys fishing and tennis and lives with his parents, dog and three older brothers in Barry, near Cardiff.

Why will the boys beat the girls?
Girls love boys! Girl power may be coming back, but we're nipping it in the bud!

What are your chances of being in the final five?
I believe in faith and I have faith in getting right to the end.

Who's been your champion on the judges?
Every one of the judges has been kind to me.

What scares you?
Spiders! They're the only thing that ever scare me.

Who do you fancy out of the girls?
I get on with Cheryl the best. We get on like brother and sister. I love her to bits.

If this fails. what's Plan B?
Try again. Easy as that. There's no point admitting defeat. If this is what your heart wants, you have to complete the challenge.

Cheryl Tweedy

Before *Popstars: The Rivals*: Since leaving school at 16, Cheryl's worked in her home town of Newcastle as a waitress, and in clubs, selling those awful 'test tube' alcohol shots. Before *Popstars: The Rivals* she was working with a producer on tracks and if you recognize her you've got an amazing memory: her TV appearances were all as a child, in things like a British Gas ad, which featured her and her brother in the bath!

Why will the girls beat the boys?
Because it's a battle of the sexes right? And the girls always win!

What are your chances of being in the final five?
Everyone's so talented and so beautiful and amazing that we all deserve it!

Who's been your champion on the judges?
Pete. Geri just stares a lot really – she's very discreet.

What scares you?
Meeting the man of my dreams, then getting hurt. When you trust someone and they cheat on you, that's not a nice feeling.

Who do you fancy out of the boys?
Jacob's not in the ten but he's a got a nice bum.

If this fails. what's Plan B?
This won't be the last you'll see of me!

Peter Smith

Why will the boys beat the girls?
We'll perform better than them, and we can sing better too. We'll give it our best shot, anyway!

What are your chances of being in the final five?
I'm confident. I know my voice is good – then again everyone's got a good voice!

Who's been your champion on the judges?
Well Louis remembers me from Irish _Popstars_.

What scares you?
I hate the idea of regretting anything, of getting old and thinking 'I wish I'd done this or that'.

Who do you fancy out of the girls?
Nadine and Sarah. Nadine is the sweetest girl alive.

If this fails, what's Plan B?
Like I say, I hate thinking of regrets, which is why I go for every opportunity. And there'll be plenty more opportunities in the future.

Before _Popstars: The Rivals_: The (ahem) 23-year-old made it down to the final 12 in Irish _Popstars_ and is still recognized around his home town of Drimnagh, near Dublin. A couple of years ago he appeared with a pre-fame Samantha Mumba in panto (he was Robin Hood to her Maid Marian!) and he was due to start a law course this year. Peter's also a born-again Christian, and has been since his mother started taking him to church ten years ago.

Kimberley Walsh

Why will the girls beat the boys?
It's about time we had another burst of Girl Power. We're hoping for some solidarity among female buyers.

What are your chances of being in the final five?
Being told I was finally in the ten was a huge shock – it makes everything else seem like a bonus.

Who's been your champion on the judges?
Louis likes everyone, but Pete's been really supportive too. I have no idea what Geri thinks. About anything.

What scares you?
Losing. And losing my family. Well and death.

Who do you fancy out of the boys?
They're all good-looking! If I was a young girl I'd be quite impressed, I believe.

If this fails, what's Plan B?
I'd go through it again because this is what I want to do. There'll be so many doors that open through this.

Before _Popstars: The Rivals_: Kimberley was in _Les Miserables_ as a youngster. She was also in CITV's _The Ward_, BBC's _Focus 2000_ (a show about a girlband which also starred Kelli from Liberty X) and _Stan The Man_ (which aired at the same time as _Popstars_, meaning Kimberley was never off the telly).
Kimberley replaces: Hazel Kaneswaren, who, as well as being pregnant, was far too ancient for the show (ie ten days), so got the boot!

Top: Happy together – though we're not too sure about Jamie's flip flop fashion atrocity

Bottom left: Chris briefs Mikey and Nikk on the morning's news. What dreadful curtains!

Bottom right: Jamie grinds an Oxo cube into Keith's hair for that fashionable gravy look

Top left: The boys' house

Top middle: Don't burn anything important, Daniel!

Top right: If all else fails, Jamie could always model for the Freemans catalogue

Main picture: A small furry animal attaches itself to Chris' chest in the world's easiest Spot The Ball competition

Bottom right: Nikk wisely declines the offer of food. Still don't like those curtains

The Girls' House

Top: How many girls does it take ...
Bottom left: Careful with that knife, Lynsey!
(Note empty wine glass)
Bottom right: Cream carpets are terribly impractical,
as Cheryl discovers

Top left: Hang on, isn't that house on Ramsey Street?

Top middle and right: You too can have a figure like Geri's. Bottoms up, Aimee!

Main pic: The girls didn't eat spaghetti bolognese that evening

Bottom: Javine with a family snap. The girls' curtains are worse than the boys'!

The twenty finalists thought the auditions were tough. And they *were* tough, in a singing-and-dancing-around kinda way. But the real work's only just begun, and over the next eight weeks, the thought of Saturday night will strike terror into these 16-24-year-olds hearts. (Kimberley has replaced pregnant Hazel, who was booted for being very ancient).

Alternating weekly between the girls and the boys, the finalists will have to choose, learn and choreograph a song, which they'll sing, absolutely live, on TV screens across the UK. The public then vote for their favourites, but there's no knowing whether the voting public will go for talent, looks or nose size. And what about the tunes? Pick the wrong song and those hopes of stardom could go out of the window. It's a big window, too, and ten of these happy faces will be stricken with misery during the course of the selection process.

The hopefuls will share their time between the high-security *Popstars* houses in the quaint Surrey suburb of Weybridge, the recording studio – the girls to Polydor, the boys to Jive – and the LWT studios on London's South Bank. And as the numbers get lower, the pressure gets higher. But let's begin with Week One: Saturday, October 12, 2002...

The boys have the unenviable task of going first in front of the voting public, but by midday on Saturday they're still in high spirits. Nikk's particularly excited by the set, 'It's just like *Stars In Their Eyes*!' he grins. Justin Timberlake's wandering around in the canteen (much to Davina's joy), and there's a sudden drama when Daniel falls through a hole in the stage and hurts his knee – but the official LWT nurse gives him the all clear.

For the afternoon dress rehearsal, the judges pile into the studio while, backstage, the boys are warming up their voices. The ten girls, lined up on a sofa in the studio, are taking notes. 'Can you hear my boys, girls?' Pete hollers. 'Yeah,' Kimberley smiles back. 'They're average.' Steady on!

Ten minutes before the show goes on air, the boys are in a state of high anxiety. Chris is joking that he needs new underwear (We hope!) and Mikey's wandering around with his shirt off. As the show goes live the boys' nerves seem to disappear – after all, it's too late to change anything now. They open with an all-singing, all-dancing version of The Beach Boys' 'I Get Around' then, one by one, they perform their songs. The verdict is positive, and the judges are impressed. There are just a couple of things: Louis reckons that, although he's good, Keith is 'not the boyband type'; and both Louis and Geri think that Chris comes across

'Look son, it doesn't matter what the judges say. What matters is what the public think.'

as being too arrogant. For the rest of the boys it's an easy show, and Jamie's bubbling over with excitement when he bounds off the stage afterwards and yells: 'That, was flippin' excellent!'

As the nation cast their votes, Andrew and Matt sit quietly on a sofa in the green room. A crestfallen Chris, meanwhile, is getting some advice from Pete. 'Look, son, it doesn't matter what the judges say. What matters is what the public think.'

'There's no bad one here among these boys,' Louis tell us. 'It's going to be difficult for the public to vote one out.' Not that difficult, as it turns out, and Andrew's the one to go.

He takes it in his stride, but Chris breaks down on stage and interrupts Davina to wail 'I've spent more time with Andrew than with anyone and he's one of the nicest people I've ever met.'

Backstage, the atmosphere is deathly. Andrew has just lost his chance at stardom, and the rest of the boys feel like they've lost their best mate.

The tunes
Keith: 'I'll Be There', The Four Tops
Chris: 'More Than A Woman', Bee Gees
Jamie: 'When You're In Love With A Beautiful Woman', Dr Hook
Daniel: 'Against All Odds', Phil Collins
Andrew: 'Hard To Say I'm Sorry', Chicago
Anton: '(It's The) Same Old Song', The Four Tops
Matt: 'Amazed', Lonestar
Nikk: 'A Little Bit More', Dr Hook
Peter: 'Since I Don't Have You', The Skyliners
Mikey: 'Drive', The Cars

'Somebody get me a gin & tonic!' booms Pete Waterman. Chris, who thought he'd be going tonight, is inconsolable. But as the tears flow and the hugs are exchanged, Louis is in the green room with his girls. He's already boasting about what great songs he's got for next week...

Tips from the top

Lawrence Johnson is vocal coach for Mis-Teeq, Samantha Mumba, Westlife and Ms Dynamite, has this advice for the boys and girls: 'You need to get a good feel for someone before you start working on the vocals. Once everyone's comfortable it's important you stay relaxed. Positive thinking and telling the truth is important, too. You'll need to sound as if someone can believe in what you're singing. I think all the vocals will grow during the course of the series – the finals shows will be vocally unrecognisable from the early ones.'

Farewell, Andrew!

'The shock of not getting through carried me through my final performance and it ended up being better than during the show! The first two weeks in the house were brilliant – it was just like being on holiday with friends. I thought that all the other boys were fantastic and we've made such good friends now, I'm not sure how I managed to hold it together. I don't know yet what I'll be doing next, but I won't give up, not at all. I want to go away for a couple of weeks and get some sun, I think!'

('Well Shane's single,' Louis muses), and Emma suddenly recalls the embarrassment of accidentally bumping into Tom Jones. 'Okay, ladies,' hollers singing tutor Lawrence, 'let's do it!'

Amid the calm of their vocal warm-ups, Nicola emits a world-class belch. 'Five minutes!' shouts a runner. A look of panic runs across every face. They huddle. 'You've got to go up a gear,' warns Lawrence. 'Cool's not good enough. Be focused. Some of you have been training for this for years – this is your chance. This will happen, if you work hard enough.' Then suddenly... They're on.

The real show absolutely whizzes by for the girls – some cope better with their songs than others and Pete's comments about Sarah ('Too tough, wrong song') bring a barrage of panto boos from the audience, while both Pete and Geri agree that Emma's song is wrong. 'I feel sorry for you,'

'Three ONE! THREE CHUFFIN' ONE!!!' The tranquility of the *Popstars* canteen is pierced by the foghorn-flavoured tones of Pete Waterman. The footie's going in his favour. In Studio One it's glamorama as the girls parade their frocks for the rehearsals, while Davina takes the opportunity to grab the girls' rivals Jamie and Nikk. 'Make sure you find the girls,' she says, 'and tell them not to worry. You've been through it, boys, only you can understand.'

The worry's certainly showing. 'Some girls look like they're about to go into the lions' den rather than a TV show!' Pete booms. 'Louis – tell them to smile a bit!'

Smiling advice is one thing we'll be hearing a lot of today – new girl Nicola spends most of her time looking as if she's just been kicked out of a band, rather than brought in as a replacement. 'You don't have to smile with your mouth,' Davina advises. 'You can smile with your eyes, too.' As the rehearsals end, Davina goes all motherly. 'Aw,' she announces affectionately, 'they're my bitches!'

Thirty minutes before the show goes live, and the girls are really strung out. 'Oh my God!' Emma suddenly realizes. 'My family's all here!' Nicola's begging Louis to let her meet Westlife

> **'Some girls look like they're about to go into the lions' den rather than a TV show!'**

The tunes

Sarah: 'Build Me Up Buttercup', The Foundations
Kymberley: 'Baby Can I Hold You', Tracy Chapman
Chloe: 'Where Do Broken Hearts Go?', Whitney Houston
Nicola: 'River Deep, Mountain High', Ike & Tina Turner
Aimee: 'Never Had A Dream Come True', S Club 7
Nadine: 'Show Me Heaven', Maria McKee
Cheryl: 'Now That I've Found You', The Foundations
Lynsey: 'All Around The World', Lisa Stansfield
Emma: 'You Might Need Somebody', Randy Crawford
Javine: 'Natural Woman', Aretha Franklin

Pete adds. Backstage, Emma and Sarah are devastated by the comments, but they're reminded – as the boys were last week – that it's not the judges who are voting. It's the public... And the public vote Lynsey out of the contest. Emma bursts into tears immediately while, on the coach, the lucky ones hug each other and begin to sob.

Even the boys begin to bawl backstage, and for an hour after the show, there's a severe mascara crisis. 'And we've just heard the news about next week,' gulps Nikk. 'They'll be voting two of us out.'

Tips from the top

Shoela Currey, Naturopath at The Vitality Centre, London has some good advice on how to stay healthy while living a busy popstar life: 'They won't have much time to eat, but they'll need to make sure they get a decent diet. They should try to eat naturally coloured foods – tomato soup with beans, carrots and courgettes is a good example – and eat according to season, with stews in the winter and salads in the summer. Nuts are good for skin, and they must have some form of breakfast, like porridge which will set them up well. Basic supplements are a good idea, too – for the popstar lifestyle I'd recommend vitamins A, C and E.'

Farewell, Lynsey!

'I'm blaming the shoes – I had to wear Javine's! No, seriously, they're all fantastic girls. I'll miss them all but Nadine and Kimberley particularly, and Aimee. I always prepare myself for the worst and I did have a feeling I'd be off, but this is only the beginning for me and there are more directions to take. This was my first ever audition and some of these girls have been slogging it out for years, so they deserve to be there.'

Week Three 26 October

1pm and crowds of fans are already gathered outside the studios waiting for their new pop idols. Jamie seems the most popular – according to one banner he's a 'Shaw thing', but it's Nikk and Matt who are out signing their new popstar autographs with their fans at the moment. 'You can't do a pun on my surname,' grumps Nikk.

During the afternoon rehearsals, Pete and Louis are already at each other's throats. 'Better than the girls,' bellows Pete. Louis is on his toes. 'The *Reynolds* Girls, perhaps,' he fires back, recalling one of Pete's less celebrated 80s creations. Before the live show, Pete and the boys get into a huddle. They're already discussing band names but, as Pete's explaining, most have already gone. 'Boys, Boyz, Da Boyz, they've all gone,' he storms. Keith's got an idea. 'Call us The Sempletones, whether I'm in the band or not!' Hm...

He may have already decided he's out, but Chris has stuffed a good luck teddy down his boxers nonetheless, which, if it doesn't bring him conventional luck, may at least influence the voting of female viewers. Five minutes before showtime and the boys are harmonizing – Jamie and Nikk lying on the floor, eyes closed with their heads on video cassettes – as vocal tutor Jo whispers words of encouragement.

As for the show itself – well, for most, it goes smoothly. But Nikk comes in for criticism: 'not great,' says Louis to

widespread boos, but Nikk bounces back when Geri praises his nice bone structure (eh?!). When the show ends the boys are left with an hour to bite their nails and listen to *Pop Idol* failure Jessica Garlick holding court backstage.

Nobody's prepared for what happens on the results show. Two boys are going tonight but before Davina can get to the first unlucky name, Peter Smith steps forward. And, live on national TV, admits the terrible truth: 'I'm two months too old to be in the band.' Nobody can believe it's happening – least of all the boys in the band, who had no idea. Pete Waterman

Peter Smith steps forward. And, live on national TV, admits the terrible truth.

chokes back his own tears. Davina starts to cry. And Peter, for one last time, performs on *Popstars: The Rivals*. After that bombshell, the announcement that the public have voted Nikk out of the show falls on slightly deaf ears, but it's no less sad. Tonight the *Popstars* boys have lost two of their most charismatic members.

And if anybody thought the first week's post-show

The tunes
Daniel: 'Celebration', Kool & The Gang
Matt: 'Everything I Own', Bread
Nikk: 'Will You Still Love Me Tomorrow?', The Crystals
Keith: 'Over My Shoulder', Mike & The Mechanics
Anton: 'Cherish', Kool & The Gang
Jamie: 'I Only Have Eyes For You', Art Garfunkel
Chris: 'Every Breath You Take', The Police
Peter: 'I Just Called To Say I Love You', Stevie Wonder
Mikey: 'I Want You Back', Jackson 5

waterworks were impressive, this week's are the Trevi Fountain of the poptelevisual world's seven wonders. In the week that follows the media will be full of doubters, but one thing beyond any doubt is the realness of these emotions. Next week had better be easier. Or Pete Waterman's heart might give out...

Tips from the top

Lisa Smosarski, Editor, Smash Hits: *'It'll be difficult for them leaving the show and going out into the real world. Everyone's scrutinizing your every move, whether it's drinking, sex, anything like that, and it only takes one step out of line for fans to turn on you. It's a tough ball game. They should try to stay strong as a unit, too – when Hear'say started arguing among themselves they essentially signed their own death certificate. The best advice, though, is don't let it go to your head, because it could all end tomorrow.'*

Farewell, Nikk!

'Everyone expected me to be really sad but I see it as a new beginning. It's a time to see how strong I am. I'm a survivor. The toughest thing's probably going to be leaving the rest of the boys behind – we've become like family over the past few weeks.'

Farewell, Peter!

'It's just something I had to do. I felt awful when Andrew had to be leaving the show the other week, because every time someone else didn't get through there was the chance they might have done if it hadn't been for me. I felt like a fraud, but I'll miss the boys and wish them all well.'

As week four rolls around, another two girls prepare to meet their destiny at the bottom of the *Popstars: The Rivals* rejection bucket. Emma seems less nervous than most, happily chatting away in the green room and explaining how she can't eat dairy products when she's singing, utilizing an elaborate metaphor which involves dropping cheese onto silk. 'Still,' she suddenly exclaims, 'has anybody tried ice cream with Smarties?'

The boys are here too – along with a smattering of their fans who are standing outside in the pouring rain for a second week. In the star-studded canteen, Daniel's just spotted crinkly rocker Paul Weller. 'Oh man!' he bellows, 'Weller is my absolute hero!' The *Popstars* team let Weller's kids in to watch the rehearsals, where we find Davina telling the boys off for distracting the girls during their performances. Between run-throughs, the girls have their picture snapped. 'We're going to look confident in this pic,' states Emma in a feat of mind over matter. 'But I'm not confident!' pipes Nicola, 'I'm terrified!' Nadine, meanwhile, is more concerned about her rather revealing top. She knows better than to take the advice of Jamie, which

What Chloe's gran knows is what the judges have spent the whole series denying...

is that it's fine. 'I'm going to the toilet to tape my boobs up!' she announces. Things are less easily solved for Sarah. She's heard that tomorrow's papers include a kiss 'n' tell from one of her exes, and Davina has to step in for a heart-to-heart.

Now, who's this vision of beauty, breasts very nearly on show, breezing down the *Popstars* gangway? It's Geri, of course, with lovable dog Harry tarted up in what the undisputed princess of pop terms a 'bling bling' diamante collar. Sadly even this posh accessory doesn't grant it access to the studio. 'Health and safety,' barks a health and safety man. But guess what? When the live show goes on air, there's Harry, perched on the seat right next to La Halliwell...

The tunes

Javine: 'Lets Stay Together', Al Green
Cheryl: 'You're Still The One', Shania Twain
Chloe: 'Rescue Me', Aretha Franklin
Emma: 'Be My Baby', The Ronettes
Nicola: 'Shout', Lulu
Aimee: 'I Only Wanna Be With You', Dusty Springfield
Kimberley: 'Unbreak My Heart', Toni Braxton
Sarah: 'Anyone Who Had A Heart', Dusty Springfield
Nadine: 'Fields Of Gold', Sting

Emma's undoubtedly the star of tonight's show. When Geri criticizes her she fires back a ballsy: 'Well, I deserve to be here', and she refuses to take criticism from Pete, either. But the voting public don't agree and Emma doesn't get through to the next round. Chloe didn't agree with the judges either – Pete told her, 'You should never have attempted that song' – and is the second (and fortunately last) of tonight's girls to wave goodbye. In the corridor after the show, Pete Waterman comes face to face with Chloe's gran. She's not happy – in fact she takes the opportunity to start yelling at him and whacking him with her handbag to the point where people have to pull her away. What Chloe's gran knows is what the judges have spent the whole series denying: it does matter what they say. And tonight, the judge's criticism has extinguished two more chances of chart superstardom.

Farewell, Chloe!
'I'm OK about it. I don't feel wonderful and all happy, but at the end of the day, that's how it's meant to be and it'll be a while yet before you see me back waitressing. This is just the beginning!'

Farewell, Emma
'I'm still very proud of myself and I think that's why I bit back. I'm not lucky to be here, I deserve to be here, I worked my hardest to be here. I hadn't felt confident the previous week but this week I was confident – and I'm confident I'll be back. It's not over yet!'

Tips from the top
Maria Killoran, TV Astrologer: 'They need to remember who they really are – if you manipulate your astral chart then your aura and your energy collapse. One or two of this lot are quite vulnerable to that. They must know that some days are full of grief, others full of happiness, and that this is because of the position of the planets. Some days you need to grow, others you need to stay where you are, and ultimately, they will always be what their destiny says they will be.'

A week since his assault with a non-deadly handbag, Pete's back on form in the LWT canteen, where we find Chris buzzing from a close encounter with Mariah Carey. 'I saw her,' he giggles, 'I went "Mariah!", and I kissed her on the cheek!' As if the stropsome R&B diva hasn't had a traumatic enough year!

This week the boys are in relaxed mode. Anton, who's been nicknamed 'Antonetron' by the boys ('cos he never misses a note) is the very embodiment of the chilled out entertainer, explaining that last night's final night - for one of the boys, at least - in the *Popstars* house was a low-key affair. It's certainly strange that while the pressure should be even tighter this week, the boys' nerves are at the lowest so far.

Since tonight's big opener finds the boys in full band mode for a version of Prince's '1999', the boys are whiling away the hours on their instruments. 'I want to learn saxophone too!' announces Keith out of the blue. 'Sax and guitar are the only instruments you can make scream!' Keith clearly does not live next door to an eight –year-old child attempting to learn the recorder. Outside, Matt's pocket of followers are all wearing personalized t-shirts with his face on. When Mikey ventures out to see, he finds himself being interrogated as the die-hard Popstars fans quiz him on his memory. 'What's my name? WHAT'S MY NAME?!?' Sensibly, he beats a hasty retreat to the safety of the green room. It's here that we find Pete and the band huddled, conspiratorially, in the corner, discussing the top secret song they're recording for the boys' first single. They've also decided on a band name. 'One True Voice,' Pete whispers. 'Though we've got to check all the legal stuff first!' Matt bursts in. 'I've been swarmed by fans! I am LOVING it!' Pete raises an eyebrow. 'Give it a few months, son. See if you love it then.' Matt's still over the moon. 'I'm 17! I'll never get bored of it!'

For the third time in a row, the judges turn against Chris. 'I hope for your sake you were happy with your song,' says Pete. 'He's not going to make the band,' says Louis. 'He doesn't have that *je ne sais quoi*,' adds Geri, prompting Chris' mum, picked out by the TV cameras, to mouth 'that bitch'. Chris looks like his world's over. But the public will decide, and when they do cast their votes it's a shock for

'The wrong boy's gone tonight... the wrong boy has definitely gone'.

The tunes
Matt: 'Pray', Take That
Mikey: 'Hello', Lionel Ritchie
Daniel: 'For Once In My Life', Stevie Wonder
Keith: 'Sorry Seems To Be The Hardest Word', Elton John
Anton: 'You Can't Hurry Love', The Supremes
Chris: 'If You Don't Know Me By Now', Harold Melvin
Jamie: 'Working My Way Back To You', Detroit Spinners

everyone. Fourth boy to leave the band is Mikey Green, who for some reason can't stop smiling when he gets the news. Just as well someone's laughing, because everyone else is in tears. 'This is awful, innit,' says ex-Take That heart-throb Mark Owen, who's milling around backstage. 'The pressure's terrible on the boys. But I think they're all great.'

'The wrong boy's gone tonight,' Pete Waterman says, with a shake of the head. 'The wrong boy has definitely gone.'

Tips from the top

Chloe Richardson: Stylist for Five, Samantha Mumba, Abs etc rcommends the following for a consistently cool look: 'When they're shopping they need to think about what they like about their body and work to show those features off. They need to find something that suits their shape, and spend a long time in front of the mirror. It doesn't matter whether it cost £10 or £100, it still hast to fit. You can mix high street fashions with designer stuff for a balance – and accessorizing is great too with belts, earrings and bits and bobs. If you're feeling comfortable, the confidence really shows.'

Farewell, Mikey!

'I'm sorry it's the end of the line but at the same time I'm so grateful for everything that's happened. I was grateful to have great food and a great place to stay and everyone running around for me and making me feel like a star. I haven't cried and I don't think I will. I'm disappointed to be out but I'm not disappointed in myself - I've come too far to be upset and I'm proud of my achievement. I've lost to the best and because of that it's hard to be upset.'

'I had a dream last night,' Davina booms across a busy rehearsal studio. 'There were dead bodies dropping onto my roof and my bed was covered in their blood!' As cheery omens go that's perhaps not what the *Popstars* girls need right now: after the shock of having to wave goodbye to Chloe and Emma last time, yet another member has to go tonight.

In what has become a recurring theme for the girls, Cheryl is preoccupied by the fear that her outfit for tonight's performance – a tiny black corset – could spring open at a moment's notice. Much 'tit tape' is applied though, as Kimberley advises her, 'Cheryl, if you've got it, flaunt it.'

Fresh from the rehearsals, Nicola blusters into the green room and catches sight of Chris' new tinted hair. 'My God' she squeals, no doubt still high on the excitement of attending last week's Westlife album launch party, 'YOU'RE GINGER!' Chris reckons it's more a case of strawberry blonde, 'and anyway, you can hardly talk!' He has a point. As the girls practice vocal warm-ups, the boys mill around in the corridor. 'Can you hear that?' whispers Matt, sneakily. 'Know what that sound is? That's the sound of CHRISTMAS NUMBER TWO! Ha ha! Loooo-sers!' Well, Matt, we'll have to wait and see about that... Javine's the star of tonight's live show, and may earn a place in history as one

'I'll miss her more than words. I just want to mother her.'

of the few people ever to silence Pete Waterman. Having been told by the godfather of pop that her song, Boyz II Men's 'End Of The Road' is a man's song, Javine answers back with a swift 'You're only saying that because Anton wanted to sing it next week'. Touché! Otherwise the judges find it difficult to find fault with anybody - and chatting with the girls after the show the nerves are incredible. For some reason, Keith chooses this moment to put Gaffa tape over his mouth.

The voting is the tightest of the entire series, and by the time lines close there are just 1,218 votes between Cheryl, who stays in the show, and Aimee, who must now leave *Popstars: The Rivals*. She bursts into tears immediately, and barely holds it together enough to sing her song for one final time. 'I'll miss her more than words,' Sarah weeps as the credits roll. 'I just want to mother her.' Fortunately, Aimee's real mum's here instead – waiting backstage with a bouquet and the rest of the Kearsleys. Aimee's in the next room being interviewed for *Popstars Extra* on ITV2. Every time she's asked a question, she bursts into tears again. It's a sombre end to the day but six boys sitting nervously in the green room are already thinking

The tunes
Nadine: 'When I Fall In Love', Nat King Cole
Kimberley: 'Emotion', The Bee Gees
Nicola: 'Wind Beneath My Wings', Bette Midler
Aimee: 'You Keep Me Hanging On', The Supremes
Sarah: 'I'll Be There', The Jackson 5
Cheryl: 'Nothing Compares 2 U', Prince
Javine: 'End Of The Road', Boyz II Men

seven days ahead. One week from now, the final lineup of the boyband will be known...

Tips from the top

Stephanie Hardwick, music industry accountant has some serious advice for the bands: 'Pop acts tend to make most of their money from touring and merchandise, and the bands won't actually receive any royalties from their Christmas singles until September 2003. When the money does come in, they need to save about 40% of it for tax and my advice would be to think of the long term. I'm not a big fan of pensions but they should definitely buy property – and try to buy it outright so they don't have a mortgage. And they should keep all their receipts for tax – popstars can claim back on everything from hi-fis to clothes!'

Farewell, Aimee!

'The past few months have been amazing and I've enjoyed everything from the singing on the show to meeting my fans, either the ones who hang around outside the studio or the ones I meet in webchats and who give themselves names like 'Number1Aimeefan'. You'll be seeing more of me in the future and the show has taught me a lot, but I'm not sure now whether I could go through all that again. You get so close to people, like I have done with these girls. I wish them all the luck in the world.'

It doesn't seem like two months since we joined ten boys here at LWT for the first time. In the intervening weeks we've waved goodbye to Andrew, Nikk, Peter, and Mikey. A pretty good group between them – and tonight, they may well get their fifth member.

The backstage atmosphere is suspiciously relaxed: Jamie teases Cheryl over her eyebrows (she's worried they're uneven, he points out they're too pointy as well, Cheryl gives him a mouthful), while Daniel's waving his arms around trying to put Anton off as he runs through 'I Believe I Can Fly'. The song goes down particularly well with Davina, who belts out her own intriguing version. 'Anton!' she barks, 'if you get ill tonight I'll take your place!' But who would host the show? It would be like a rudderless ship crashing on the rocks of TV insanity!

For the live show, we see Louis issuing a call for the entire population of Wales to support Matt, and we see Geri deciding that Chris 'must definitely go through'. There are no bad performances tonight, and as the public cast their votes, the backstage area is busy, but calm. Perhaps it's the eye of the storm. Davina's waving Bagpuss socks around and Matt's furiously texting on his phone - not voting for himself, surely? Five minutes before they're back on air, Pete's dragging his boys into a huddle for some last

> **'Chris doesn't cry. He doesn't break down. He bows out like a true pro'**

minute encouragement. 'These boys have worked harder than anyone I've ever seen in my life,' Pete explains to anyone who'll listen. 'And there are no losers tonight.' Just in case, TV psychologist Dr Raj Persaud has been drafted in, and he's on counselling standby.

This week the results show is different. Rather than sending each of the boys to sit on the sofa when they're safe, there are five stools on the stage: instant Westlife. Keith's the first to find out he's safe; he takes his seat. Then Matt, who's in tears, joins him. Then Daniel, then Anton. There's one stool left, but two boys. Jamie and Chris meet Davina in the centre of the stage. Jamie begins to look very ill indeed, but Chris seems calm. And the final boy to leave *Popstars: The Rivals* is... Chris. He doesn't cry. He doesn't break down. He thanks everyone who's supported him and then sings his song better than he's ever sung it before. He bows out like a true pro.

In the green room, Dr Raj has just heard that the boys are called One True Voice. 'Chris is probably happy he's not in the band with a name like that!' he chuckles. Then it's off to the bar for a celebration, and a chance for Pete's male vocal

The tunes
Jamie: 'Everyday Hurts', Sad Café
Anton: 'I Believe I Can Fly', R Kelly
Chris: 'With A Little Help From My Friends', The Beatles
Keith: 'You Are So Beautiful, Joe Cocker
Daniel: 'Candle In The Wind', Elton John
Matt: 'I'll Be There For You', The Rembrandts

harmony group to hug their friends, each other and anyone else who comes near them! One True Voice have precisely one week in which to relax. After that, the girl group will be unveiled. And then it's war...

Tips from the top

Mark Frith, Editor of Heat *magazine has this to say about fame: 'Fame is fleeting, and from now on the bands will have to earn the right to longevity. The only way to deal with fame is to treat it like a job. A job with terrible hours, but the bands should make sure they keep their real life separate and don't lose sight of it. In terms of the paparazzi, they shouldn't feel concerned about being photographed while they're out, but they should make initial enquiries with Pete and Louis to see what sort of behaviour is acceptable.'*

Farewell, Chris!

'Obviously I'm disappointed, but if I'd got into the band then it would have been at the expense of Jamie, and he deserves his place. If they're up for it I'd love to form a band with the other boys, but like I said right at the start I've got plans B, C, D, E... I've got more up my sleeve after this. It's been an absolute honour to be involved with the show this far – and I wish the lads all the best with the single. I hope they wish me luck in the new year, too!'

It's been a strange week for the Rivals bands. The girls – who've now settled on the name Girls Aloud – have paid a visit to a children's cancer hospital, while the boys have shot the videos for their double A-side and, just last night, flooded their kitchen after a certain boy, who shall remain nameless, left the upstairs taps on and managed to bring down a ceiling or two.

Steering clear of basins, Jamie's sneaked into the studio to watch the girls' rehearsal, Jamie's evaluating Louis' comments on a backstage monitor. 'I'd like to have a six piece, because there's not one I'd get rid of' Louis says. 'Rubbish!' announces Jamie. Does he know something we don't? For most of the run-throughs, Matt sits down with us and provides a running commentary of each girl's performance. 'She was flat in that chorus'. 'She sounds great, but I'm not sure about the dress.' 'She's brilliant.' 'She's fit.'

This week's songs are an upbeat selection – dancefloor classics of yesteryear like 'I'm So Excited' and 'I Wanna Dance With Somebody', a song which Nadine reckons 'is gonna kill me if I have to sing it too often!' (Hopefully just the one performance tonight, then.) Then there's 'Holding Out For A Hero', the signature tune of old rock chick Bonnie Tyler: during the rehearsal, Sarah misses one of her notes. Everyone thought it was

'What a way to end the series ... I really don't know what happened'

an intentional homage to Tyler's own vocal technique, but Sarah bursts into tears, and is inconsolable for the rest of the afternoon, despite Davina's best attempts to calm her down.

'There's going to be extreme happiness and extreme sadness,' predicts Pete Waterman, the voice of experience and the king of stating the bleeding obvious. But, like last week, you'd be hard picked to find anybody prepared to actually predict the girl to go. The show doesn't clear things up, either – the girls are all on good form. Some better than others, but nobody's bad; no bum notes from Sarah, no harsh words from the judges. As the phonelines open it really is impossible to guess who'll be the one to go.

Throughout the series, Javine Hylton, has stood head and shoulders above every other girl on that stage, her effortless performances and strong will showcasing a star not in the making, but a star who's already made. Somehow, by a freak of public idiocy, she gets the least votes. The girls are all in tears – perhaps not for Javine, but due to a combination of

The tunes
Sarah: 'Holding Out For A Hero', Bonnie Tyler
Nadine: 'I Wanna Dance With Somebody', Whitney Houston
Kimberley: 'Chain Reaction', Diana Ross
Nicola: 'I'm So Excited', The Pointer Sisters
Javine: 'I'm Every Woman', Whitney Houston
Cheryl: 'Right Here Waiting', Richard Marx

shock and the realization that Girls Aloud have lost a key member. Backstage there's a stunned silence. 'What a way to end the series,' Pete muses. 'I really don't know what happened.' But one thing's for sure – the boys think their path to Number One now has one less obstacle...

Tips from the top

Scott Mills, Radio One DJ: 'This will be the hardest they'll ever have to work. Getting in at 1am and getting up at 5am and doing all these shows will be difficult. But the thing I'll be interested in is whether they're good interviewees – a lot of people are dull because they're so trained. Britney Spears and Ricky Martin are so boring to interview. Liberty X are great – they've been trained but they can twist it so an interview is always fresh. Oh, and I don't want to have to play cover versions. I'm bored of that and I think everyone else is.'

Farewell, Javine!

'I was so nervous tonight – the most nervous I've been throughout the whole series – 'cos people were building me up to be this huge singer, and it was difficult to meet those expectations. It hasn't really sunk in yet. I wouldn't say I was shocked, exactly, and I did want to be in the band, but at the end of the day I have confidence in myself and I will be a success. Obviously I'm going to miss the girls – I've made really good friends, and one or two of them are people with whom I'll stay friends forever. I'm not going to cry – I just want to get to the bar!'

Nadine Coyle

Own up. Louis wanted you in the band all along, didn't he?
'Um...' (Long pause as she attempts to rephrase the word 'Yes') 'Well, I think he would have liked me in the band. I think I proved myself at each step, though.'

How much help has Geri been?
'Personally? Er... I haven't had any career advice from her. I've never even had a conversation with her – I've only really heard her speak when she's commenting on the TV show.'

The *Derry Journal* have gone a bit bonkers for you...
'Yeah! They've really got behind me and I haven't even had a chance to go back there yet, but everyone says they've been really supportive. They' sent me messages after the show and stuff.'

Are you glad the original Nicola went?
'I think she felt intimidated or something – when you spoke to her she'd blush or try to end it as soon as possible... Maybe she just didn't like me!'

Have you spoken to Aimee much since she left?
'Yeah I speak to her a lot – she's doing fine and she'll do fine. She's such a nice girl – so sweet. Oh God, it's hard. I really did think she was going to be in the band. When we were in the house everyone had their fantasy band lineup and Aimee was on everybody's list.'

What happens if you go to Number Two?
'I would be absolutely over the moon. I'm 17, I've just left school, and even to have the chance to record a song, or shoot a video, I mean that's an honour. It sounds clichéd but it's true. Of course, having a Number One wouldn't hurt!'

Read all about it
Nadine's boyfriend, Neil McCafferty, plays for Charlton Athletic FC. It looks like Nadine and Neil are on their way to becoming the Irish Posh and Becks.

Vital statistics
Age: 17 **From:** Derry
Date of birth: June 15, 1985
Number One when born:
'You'll Never Walk Alone', The Crowd
Starsign: Gemini **Height:** 5'6"
What the fans say: 'Persistent, talented and friendly – I love her!' (Danielle, 17)

Girls Aloud

Sarah Harding

Happy to be in?
'I'm ecstastic!'

Good. You celebrated your birthday during November - what did you do?
'Well it was a bit awkward because it was Aimee's leaving day, but I just went out with my mum – went down the Bentall Centre! So I'll be having a postponed birthday after all this. I bought a new phone.'

Well we hope you got it insured.
'Oh God, I can't believe you said that – I was at Waterloo Station one week later and I managed to drop it right down the stairs – boing, boing, boing down the steps! But yes, it was insured – just in case I, er, dropped it down the stairs, ha!'

What was your best song of the series?
'I'll Be There', definitely. I know that song inside and out. 'Build Me Up Buttercup' was good, too, because it reflected my personality.'

You had a bit of a tough time with the press. Did it affect you?
'I got to the point where I just let it wash over me. Look how far I've come - if people had listened to that crap I would have been gone a long time ago. You shouldn't believe what you read in the papers because at the end of the day people will do anything for money, because they're sick.'

What have been your highlights?
'I love it when we have the 'Come on the girls!' attitude, but the best moment was when Chloe, Javine and I went busking. We got £22! But the boys got £60 – we so thought we'd whoop their ass! Haha! It was so funny.'

Read all about it
Sarah had to have a nose job after she broke it in an accident. She's got no plans to go under the knife again, though, which is just as well 'cos she's perfect just as she is!

Vital statistics
Age: 21 **From:** Cheshire
Date of birth: November 17, 1981
Number One when born:
'Every Little Thing She Does Is Magic', The Police **Starsign:** Scorpio
Height: 5'6" **What the fans say:**
'Overcame loads to be here, really happy for her!' (Nicole, 16)

Nicola Roberts

The songs you sang were great – did you choose them?

'Well "River Deep Mountain High" was actually chosen for the Nicola who left, and I liked it, but I'm better at ballads than fast songs. When they gave me "Shout" I loved it but I was like "Shout? WHAT?!?". I got a ballad the next week though. Then the final week, singing "I'm So Excited" was perfect.'

Was the Westlife party the highlight of your year?

'Oh yeah. But I did love doing the Saturday shows too. The only reason I enjoyed them is because I got through, though, haha! The atmosphere was just electric. And being on *cd:UK* was great too – we did Eat my Goal which was quite embarrassing to be honest.'

Which of your AA-side songs do you prefer?

'I prefer "Sound Of The Underground". Definitely! It's just a boss song! It's upbeat, it's got a brilliant bassline to it, it's got loads of attitude and a great routine – it's really interesting to watch because I think the public are going to expect us to come out with some cheesy pop thing.'

What was it like watching the girls start without you?

'It was nice in a way because I'd had time with my family – a lot of the girls came straight out of the auditions and into the house. But the first week when they were on TV I was just sat at home watching it on the telly almost in tears! Then I finally got in. Now here I am!'

Describe the experience so far?

'Crazy! And fast! One of Cheryl's favourite phrases – it's an emotional rollercoaster. Crazy. Mad! Brilliant, like!'

Read all about it

Louis' boys, Westlife, and his girls, Girls Aloud, are getting on like a house on fire! Nicola and Sarah certainly made an impression on Mark and Kian respectively!

Vital statistics

Age: 18 **From:** Runcorn
Date of birth: October 5, 1984
Number One when born:
'Careless Whisper', George Michael
Starsign: Libra **Height:** 5'4"
What the fans say: 'Looks nice even when she's not smiling!' (Duncan, 13)

Girls Aloud

Cheryl Tweedy

Describe the past five months.
'Madness. But in a good way. To come from selling cocktail drinks in a nightclub to having a chance of being Number One – if that's not madness I don't know what is!'

Tell us about your corset problems.
'Well when I first tried it on it was too big. So they said they'd get it taken in, but then it was too tight and I could not breathe! So they took it back out again... But when I moved my arms I could feel myself coming out! So I got tit tape all over me, but they still came out! When I was on stage I was frightened to move! Horrible!'

Have you had loads of support back home?
'Newcastle went Cheryl beserk! Newcastle are also the best football supporters – they're good at cheering people on. It's a run down area, and for me to come from nothing to doing this... Well, they're really proud.'

Are you going to move to London?
'I'm going to buy a flat in Newcastle, of course! Hopefully I'll have enough money to get one in London too but I'll definitely get one up there, it's still my home.'

Did the press stories get to you?
'I just laughed, because if you didn't laugh you'd cry. And what's the point in crying? People are reading it, but it's all forgotten so soon. It's fish and chip paper the next day, so who cares.'

Best night out...
'Westlife party. Actually I'm lying – when me, Javine, Sarah and Chloe went out for a drink near the house and drank three bottles of red wine between us! Haha! Hilarious!'

Read all about it
Rumours abound about Cheryl's love life! She's especially close to Jacob, but she certainly enjoyed her boogie with Gareth Gates at the infamous Westlife album party...

Vital statistics
Age: 19 **From:** Newcastle
Date of birth: June 30, 1983
Number One when born:
'Every Breath You Take', The Police
Starsign: Cancer
Height: 5'4"
What the fans say: 'Absolutely gorgeous, top bird' (Andy, 19)

Kimberley Walsh

What was it like stepping into the group at a later stage?
'It wasn't too bad because they'd only been in there a week or so and I'd kept in contact with Nadine and Cheryl.'

What's your high point so far?
'Ooh, just each week getting through, it's like getting over another hurdle and it means that you've achieved something else.'

Who's your favourite out of the boys?
'Daniel was my favourite all along, as an all-rounder he's the strongest and I think you can see the passion. That's why the audience connected with him, because they could see how much he wanted it and how much he was enjoying it.'

Do you think the judges were fair on the girls?
'I think they were. I think they just tried to speak the truth, and speak their minds without being unnecessarily rude. They've never insulted anybody's appearance or personality, they've just talked about the music. It's hard enough as it is without criticism!'

Who's been the rowdiest in the house?
'Nicola's probably the loudest. Well, since Chloe left anyway! It's the red hair, you see. But in a good way!'

Still reckon you'll be Number One at Christmas?
'We've got an amazing single. It's all about character – we're going to put more personality across in our song than the boys and hopefully people will get that vibe from us. The songs are brilliant as well.'

Which do you prefer?
'"Sound Of The Underground". It really is a good song. It's a bit more "now". I think "Stay Another Day" will have bells on it, though, which will be good for Christmas.'

Read all about it
Kimberley has some very famous supporters. Samia Ghadie who plays Corrie's Maria Sutherland said, 'I voted for Kimberley each Saturday. I hoped she'd make it into the band.'

Vital statistics
Age: 21 **From:** Bradford
Date of birth: November 20, 1981
Number One when born:
'Every Little Thing She Does Is Magic', The Police **Starsign:** Scorpio
Height: 5'5"
What the fans say: 'Wish my skin was as perfect as hers!' (Harriet, 18)

Anton Gordon

Do you reckon you had the height advantage?
'Ha! I actually thought it would be a disadvantage to start with because I stand out too much and look like an individual rather than a band member. But it's gone alright for me!'

What does everyone back home reckon to your being a popstar?
'Where I'm from, not a lot of people become big stars so I've become a role model! I don't come from a lush life but we've had all we need to survive, and the life I've lived is what's made me today.'

What's the best advice you were given?
'Pete Waterman told me just to enjoy it – he said "It's the best opportunity you've ever been given. Make the most of it". And I did!'

You had a chat with Keisha from the Sugababes when they came down – what did she say?
'I spoke to her for a long time. She said her mum was behind me and that I should just keep on going and be myself. That was great coming from a celebrity like her. For her to say that to me meant an awful lot.'

What do you say to the critics of the show?
'They say it's cruel because it's hurting our feelings, but we knew what it was going to be when we applied for it. Not everyone's going to like the show but we're here for the people who do.'

Is it hard work to make singing look so effortless?
'Luckily that's just the way my voice is, and the way I perform. I'm quite a laid back kind of person so if it seems it's effortless, I'm still working hard!

Why are you going to beat the girls?
'Our music's better!'

Read all about it
Pete calls Anton his silent but deadly weapon, and with his sublime voice and quiet manner you can see why. And he's got pop pedigree too: his cousin is Coree from Damage.

Vital statistics
Age: 19 **From:** Neasden, London
Date of birth: June 30, 1983
Number One when born:
'Every Breath You Take', The Police
Starsign: Cancer
Height: 6'2"
What the fans say: 'He's the gentle giant!' (Tanya, 12)

One True Voice

Matt Johnson

What's the best advice you were given?

'You get lots of advice as you go through something like this but near the beginning someone told me, 'You never get a second chance to make a first impression'. I always tried to remember that.'

So what was the first impression you made on the boys?

'Well, I held myself back from everyone a bit because that's just what I'm like – I like to watch people for a while and weigh them up. Then I jump right in the deep end!'

You were really upset about Peter Smith quitting – was it a surprise?

'I didn't even know what was happening. He was saying things to us beforehand like "You know that I'll never forget you". Then during the results show, because I was sat there on the couch, I couldn't hear properly! Then he said he was two months too old and I thought he just meant, y'know, spiritually or something. It was unbelievable, but a major TV moment!'

Do you still speak to him?

'Yeah, I'm still in contact with him. We text each other all the time. He's cool. He did what he thought was the best thing for the band.'

What did you think of the single when you first heard it?

'Pete played it to me really early on to see what I thought of it – fortunately I said it was good! When I found out that the Gibb brothers had written it I just couldn't believe it – my mum was a really big Bee Gees fan and it's a massive honour.'

What are you going to do with your money?

'Pete told us to take half of everything we get paid and put it in the bank for the tax man!'

Read all about it

Poor Matt often found himself on the wrong end of a practical joke. Keith said, 'We play pranks on everyone, but mostly Matt, 'cos he's the youngest.'

Vital statistics

Age: 17 **From:** Chester, North Wales
Date of birth: September 10, 1985
Number One when born:
'Dancing In The Street', Mick Jagger & David Bowie
Starsign: Virgo **Height:** 5'7"
What the fans say: 'Not afraid to show his emotions!' (Maxine, 15)

Daniel Pearce

A year ago, would you have thought about being in a group like this?

'No, not at all. I was doing my gigging and my songwriting and doing quite well at it. I was actually thinking of trying to be a solo artist. But this has been so much fun – and far less work because there's four other guys!'

Is it nice that they're getting you involved with songwriting as well as singing?

'Yeah, I'm really loving the fact that people don't forget that as well as being a singer I can play drums and other instruments, and write songs too. I've got loads of songs on the go as well.'

You became quite ill during November – what happened?

'Oh God, I just sat up in bed one morning and went 'Eeuegghhg – OW!' I got worse during the day and called the doctor. He came and said "It's a kidney infection". Not what I needed at that point – but I'm alright now.

The papers said that the boys cried too much. Do you agree?

'No. People on the outside can never understand how hard it is to get up in front of 8 million people, and sing. They were real emotions coming out on those results shows. Trying to fulfill your dream is the hardest thing in the world.'

What ambitions do you have left?

'I want a couple of platinum-selling albums, and the knowledge that I've been the best I can be. It's quite simple for me. I just want respect as a musician and I'm grateful for this opportunity. And if we don't have a Number One – well, it's amazing to be in the position where that's even a possibility. That's good enough for me. And even the shittiest gig in the world is better than an office job!

Read all about it

According to the Daily Star when chart-topping Sugababes mingled with the Pop Rivals boys at one of the Saturday night shows, 17-year-old Keisha only had eyes for Daniel.

Vital statistics

Age: 24 **From:** Ashford, Kent
Date of birth: May 29, 1978
Number One when born: 'Rivers Of Babylon', Boney M
Starsign: Gemini
Height: 5'7"
What the fans say: 'Nice face and talented too' (Emma, 16)

One True Voice

Keith Semple

Did it annoy you that Louis kept saying you were too rocky for the band?

'I do agree with him in a sense, but I don't think being a bit rocky necessarily made me wrong for the band. He changed his mind in the end, anyway!'

Has pop music won you round yet?

'I've always been quite sceptical of the pop world – but my views are changing. It's a really different type of industry and I slightly miss singing live, which I used to do every three days.'

Do you wish you had more fans with banners? Jamie had loads!

'I'm not really in it for that. I'd just as soon have respect from 40-year-old men, because that's the musical background I've come from. I want respect from people who understand music, but it's great to have younger fans too.'

Tell us about some of the other boys.

'Anton's always cheering me up and he actually listens to what you say; Daniel's very easy to talk to; Matt's a real laugh; and Jamie is great fun, we get on well.

Loads of people reckon you're one of the friendliest people on the show...

'Well I do try to be nice to everybody. I can be a bit of a stroppy diva sometimes and I wasn't particularly liked at home – this show meant I could really start again. When I go back to Northern Ireland it's like you're not allowed to dream, you're not allowed to strive, and the attitude is that you grow up, get married, settle down and never leave the place. It's like you're not allowed to have thoughts, but with this you're allowed to be yourself and you're allowed to be enthusiastic.'

Read all about it

If it wasn't for Keith's grandmother, Elsie, who picked up the Pop Rivals application form for him, Keith might have disappeared into the world of rock forever!

Vital statistics

Age: 21 **From:** Larne, Northern Ireland
Date of birth: September 20, 1981
Number One when born: 'Prince Charming' by Adam Ant
Starsign: Virgo **Height:** 5'8"
What the fans say: 'I love him cos of his ears!' (Sam, 14)

Jamie Shaw

How will you make sure you last longer than Hear'say?

'Hear'say weren't friends, but we all are. We pull each other up when we're down – and we're not going to go all diva-esque, either. I treat everyone the same. Nobody deserves to be treated better than anyone else.'

You came quite close to eviction a couple of times – what was that like?

'Being almost voted out is a really weird situation to be in – and it's absolutely terrible. I'd hate to go through it again.'

What do you think of the other boys?

'I get on well with Keith; Daniel was quiet and I didn't think I'd get on with him, but I do; Matt is someone I've grown to like – I was a bit wary of him to start with; And Anton, well, he's just a lovely, easy, outgoing, nice guy.'

Who've been your biggest supporters?

'All the kids back at home at my junior school and my old teachers have been amazing. I really need to thank them – they've given me encouragement all the way through.'

Your blonde highlights disappeared during October. Why was that?

'They weren't working at all. Didn't like 'em. So we got Clifford, our new stylist, who's done Britney, J.Lo, everyone – to sort it out. He's got seven different hairstyles for me!'

Has Pete told you about steam engines yet?

'Yes! No, it's REALLY interesting! He makes them, you know! In his factory! It's fascinating – he's going to take me to his factory and show me how it's all done. I think the rest of the boys will probably give that a miss.'

Read all about it

Just a year ago, Jamie was suffering bullying at school and comfort-eating to help him through each day. So well done Jamie for not letting the bullies get the best of you!

Vital statistics

Age: 17 **From:** Cardiff
Date of birth: June 8, 1985
Number One when born:
'19', Paul Hardcastle
Starsign: Gemini
Height: 5'8"
What the fans say: 'So cute!'
(Rochelle, 17)

Pete Waterman

Happy with the final lineup?
Definitely. You've got a very different band from any other boy... (Catches himself) Er, boy act. It's been an absolutely amazing series.

Do you ever feel you were too harsh as a judge?
I think some of the editing showed me as being hard and I'm not that hard. I think it made good TV. But with the boys I think behind the scenes you've seen that I was literally their best mate, and I've tried to look after them all the way through.

Has anything gone wrong?
Not for me personally, but it's a shame the show got some bad press. At the end of the day though, I've had ten lovely boys, and a band with five lads who I'd have put money on at the start.

Would you really have predicted them?
The public have voted the way I thought they'd vote. It's interesting sometimes how people fell away then came back – for example Matt, who came back at the last minute. I've been doing this for thirty or forty years – I haven't once called it wrong on this show. It is gratifying that I can still see what the audience love and when I lose that touch maybe I should pack it in.

Do you have any favourites?
No - I've got to be all their friends. I'm their mate and their disciplinarian so I have to love them all equally. I can't lose that grip or it's all gone.

You're best known as a producer – who's managing the band?
Me! I've brought them this far. So I'll take them through every step. I've finished the two tracks thank goodness, so we're ready, and the single will shock people. It sounds nothing like anything else. What happens now is that I have to get my head down writing new songs.

Did you ever regret taking this on?
Health-wise, yes! But having such a brilliant final band makes everything worth it.

Louis Walsh

What's been your high point of the series?
Working with the whole crew. They're always amusing and interesting – and they've been really nice to me.

Was there anything that disappointed you?
I think it was when Aimee went. And I was worried Matt wouldn't get through to the boys – but he got the second biggest vote which was great.

Are you worried about the threat of One True Voice?
Pete's got a really great band. It's good for the industry and for TV, too. So there are two hit bands to come out of this - and the Cheeky Girls, who I was always hoping would beat Robbie Williams to Number One!

Do you think you were ever too tough as a judge?
Not at all. (Thinks) I was actually far too nice. I should have been more honest but people, especially in the studio, don't like you being nasty.

Do you miss Hazel, or the original Nicola?
I'm absolutely delighted the first Nicola went because it meant we had the other Nicola along in her place, who is excellent. And Hazel would have been a real asset to the band vocally, so I'm still sad she went.

You got your wish for Irish band members. Did your experience with Six in Irish Popstars help?
I think so, but we were working with 4 million people in Ireland and 60 million here at *Popstars: The Rivals* so it's a bigger pool of talent. (Thinks) Well, it's supposedly a bigger talent pool – but then you look at the bands and the best people, like Keith and Nadine, are Irish.

How long will Girls Aloud be around for?
It sounds obvious, but they'll be around for as long as they want. It's absolutely up to them from this stage onwards.

Do you have any regrets?
Absolutely not. I've especially enjoyed taking the piss out of Pete and Geri on a weekly basis, haha! I've loved every single moment of the whole series, and it's the most fun I've had in a really long time.

She has a way of singing sentences, it's magic, and she is such a mature singer.

You hosted the live final of the first *Popstars*. Are these two bands anything like Hear'say?

They're very different. Hear'say were undoubtedly very talented but I think they were chosen for television rather than for being in a band. Pete and Louis were looking for popstars. I hope these bands fare better with the press – Hear'say were an amazing phenomenon, but I wouldn't wish the backlash they got on my worst enemy. Kym Marsh did such the right thing.

What's been your one highlight of Popstars: The Rivals?

Nadine. In general. Every time she sang or opened her mouth I got the most amazing feeling. She has got the voice of an angel and it's not just the fact that she can sing in tune, it's the tone of her voice and her phrasing.

Talk us through your experience of the Peter Smith night.

I was in my dressing room. About ten minutes before we went back on air for the results show, the producer came up and said, 'There's going to be an announcement made during the show. I'm not going to tell you who's making it or why, just go with it and we'll tell you what to do in your earpiece'. In retrospect I would like to have known beforehand, and I don't think Peter should have stopped the show – as it happened it was all a bit shambolic.

Everyone was criticized for crying too much that night...

From my own perspective, I can identify with the catastrophic loss of a dream, and it makes me livid when people say they're crying for the cameras - you can't just cry on command, and what would these kids, especially the boys, gain from crying on national TV?

What was it like having to tell people they were out?

Awful. The reason I have a long pause is that I don't want to have to

'There's going to be an announcement made during the show. I'm not going to tell you who is making it or why, just go with it' *The Producer*

tell them! I don't want to be the person that has to tell them their dream is over. I only got the result in my ear ten seconds before I had to say it and it wasn't usually the person I though it would be. Aimee's name was very difficult to say because I knew she was going to take it very badly.

Was it cruel to make them sing again at the end?
When I heard about it I thought it was barbaric. But the first week, when Andrew hadn't performed that well during the show itself, he sang again and it was the best I'd ever heard him. I just thought, 'If only you'd sung like that in the show you might still be in the band'.

Have the judges been too harsh?
They were too easy on them! The tough thing is that people at home often agree, but in the studio the audience are with the boys and girls so they get booed. With someone like Pete you almost expected it because he's known as being ruthless, but with Geri it was very tough for her.

What do you think the public were voting for?
Perhaps surprisingly, I think the public were actually voting for the people who gave the best vocal performances. The public have become very picky. We only want the best – and we expect the best. But it's always a very difficult decision.

Finally, who do you think will get to Number One?
I can't say. I think I've got an idea but I can't say. I'd have to kill you. From the rumours I've heard on the street, I've got a good idea. But don't think you can wangle it out of me! I know your ploys!

Dammit. So what do you think the future holds for the ones who didn't get through? *Celebrity Big Brother*?
(Laughs) It's difficult to say. There are so many celebrities from reality TV programmes and you do wonder if there's room in the world of showbiz to accommodate all of them. But I do know that all of them are going to get something from this – even if it's just something to tell the grandchildren.

The Single

The lead track is 'Sound Of The Underground', an arms-aloft party wibbler which sounds like Destiny's Child locked in a room with Ricky Martin and recalls the heady days of Spicemania, and has nothing to do with London's subterranean tube network. The AA-side is 'Stay Another Day', a sweeping ballad which will make people cry.

Genetics

18 different girls have been Number One during 2002. Secret weapon: 'Stay Another Day' has got bells in it! And we all know what bells mean: Christmas Number One! (Or a sleepless night, if you live near a church.)
Release date: December 16, 2002

Video

The girls' video shoot took place in London just days after the final lineup was announced.
Prior to release the odds according to Ladbrokes: 4/1 for Christmas Number One. (The Cheeky Girls are 20/1, if you're wondering.)

Writer

'Stay Another Day' was originally Christmas Number One for East 17 (think Blazin' Squad with less members) in 1994 - in the end it was at the top of the charts for five weeks. 'Sound Of The Underground' was written by Brian Higgins, who was responsible for Cher's 'Believe' and the Sugababes' 'Round Round' among several hundred other pop classics.

Record label

Polydor. Louis reckons Polydor are the best pop outfit in the country – he signed Samantha Mumba to the them – and Girls Aloud will be labelmates with Eminem, S Club, Daniel Bedingfield and Dr Dre. Polydor also steered Hear'say to their record-breaking Number One debut single. Polydor scored a huge Christmas number one with Band Aid II's 'Do They Know It's Christmas?'.
The song was produced by, yes you've guessed it, Pete Waterman.

Manager

Louis Walsh. Has scored a Christmas Number One for Westlife, with 'I Have A Dream' / 'Seasons In The Sun' in 1999. Both songs were produced by (oh cruel fate!) Pete Waterman.

Producer

It's Brian Higgins – again! His production credits include Savage Garden and Dannii Minogue.

One True Voice

Single
'Sacred Trust' is an upbeat, straightforward pop number which old people may find reminds them of Kelly Marie's 80s classic 'Feels Like I'm In Love'. The AA-side is the snappily-titled 'After You're Gone (I'll Still Be Loving You)', a massive great ballad of which Westlife should be very jealous indeed.

Record label
Jive/Ebul. Ebul is actually Pete's own label – he started it with Jive in 1996 and the name stands for Eastern Block Unity Label (after he merged two labels, Eastern Block and Unity, into one chart-mauling uberlabel). One True Voice are labelmates with Britney, *NSYNC, Backstreet Boys, R Kelly and the still-glowing embers of the Steps phenomenon.

Producer
Pete Waterman. Has been responsible for producing every Number One in the charts' 50-year history. Or thereabouts ha ha!

Video
The boys shot their two videos on Monday, November 25, and Tuesday 26.
Prior to release the odds according to Ladbrokes: 4/7 for Christmas Number One. (Sir Cliff Richard is 40/1, if you're wondering.)

Writer
The Bee Gees wrote 'Sacred Trust' yonks ago and Pete's been chasing permission to adapt it for three years. During October, he finally got the green light – and the One True Voice version sounds quite different to the Bee Gees' original. Pete wrote 'After You're Gone...' with Daniel from the band, who also drums on the single.

Genetics
34 different boys have been Number One during 2002. Mind you, ten of these were the Blazin' Squad (think East 17 with more members). Secret weapon: Bee Gees fans are generally oldies with fabulously good taste who only buy one single a year – and this could be it. (Whereas most ex-East 17 fans are either in jail or pretending they never liked pop in the first place – the self-deluding fools that they are.)

Manager
Though he's best known as a pop producer, Pete's decided to manage One True Voice himself. Let's hope he'll still have time to produce the no-doubt-excellent next Geri Halliwell album!

Popstars: The Facts

Both bands recorded their singles with the final six vocalists – the unlucky sixth members' voices were whipped off at the last minute!

Strangely, Pete Waterman said he would kill himself if One True Voice didn't get to Number One!

Before Girls Aloud, Nicola was earning £3.50 per hour at her local pub. This officially counts as a pay rise!

The girls' home video collection included *Geri Yoga* and the DVD of the first *Popstars* series!

The fish & chip shop round the corner from PWL became a regular hangout for certain members of One True Voice!

The girls' hideaway home was in the same superposh Surrey estate as old rocker Cliff Richard's flash pad!

While recording a show at LWT towers, Robbie Williams popped into Matt's dressing room for a quick chat – and stayed there for half an hour!

Unexpectedly, Rolling Stone Mick Jagger has come out as a fan of the *Popstars* series!

Matt from One True Voice eats chips for breakfast, lunch and dinner. Though he once took Jamie for lunch at Pizza Hut!

After the first live show, Pete had a party for the boys at his house. It was the first time he'd had a house party – and the last

On a visit to the boys' house, Pete somehow managed to pull the toilet door off its hinges!

Danny from Hear'say sent One True Voice two bottles of champagne when they got into the band.

Daniel

Sarah

Anton

Nicola

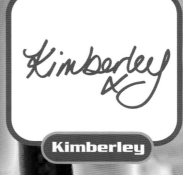

Kimberley

Cheryl

Nadine

Keith

Matt

Jamie